To D:
You are
Boldness, & humility ♡

# Hide And Seek

Love –

Denise
Ga 5:22-23

# Hide And Seek

❧

## Discovering Your Hidden Treasures

Danise C. DiStasi

Copyright © 2016, by Danise C. DiStasi  Loveland, OH 45140
All rights reserved. No part of this book may be reproduced or utilized in any way or by any means, electronic or mechanical, including photocopying, recording, or by any information storage retrieval system, without prior permission from the publisher.
Names, characters, and incidents either are the product of the author's imagination or are used fictitiously. Any resemblance to actual persons, living or dead, events, organizations, or locales is coincidental.
Danise C. DiStasi
Hide And Seek; Discovering Your Hidden/by Danise C. DiStasi
Copyedit: Becky Smith
ISBN-13: 9780692498262
ISBN-10: 0692498265 Fiction/Teaching Parable
Cover design: Jessica Shely, Creative Director & Owner, Green Pasture Designs

# Dedication

*My life has come full circle. I lovingly dedicate this special book
to my precious gifts from God, Evi Isabella and Mea Adrianna.
When I look into the eyes of these beautiful girls,
I see the awesome, mighty women of God they are destined to be.
Evi and Mea, you will move mountains. I love you both so dearly!*

*And to Marisa, this story would not be so if you hadn't been in my life.
I thank God for you each day. Matt, thank you for being the awesome
husband to my daughter and dad to my grandchildren.
And you stand alone as the wonderful young man God created you to be.*

*My heart sings as I witness in Evi and Mea the true
meaning of love, joy and peace!*

# Introduction

The year was 1972, the year of maxi dresses and miniskirts. Grease was a Broadway hit, ABBA sang "Mama Mia," and the world was abuzz with the *Roe v. Wade* debate. While President Nixon took an historic trip to China, a young woman named Belle stood holding an airline ticket, prepared to make a decision based on one little lie. That decision would forever change her life and fear, cleverly disguised as courage, became the driving force behind her determination.

And so began the vicious cycle for Belle, who buried the lie in order to prove she was an independent woman, worthy of validation, who would not be defined by the lie, by one simple act. Somewhere in her heart she desired to know she was someone of worth and value, to be known and loved, but the lie took over, and the pure treasure deep within was buried.

Years later, what the world saw in Belle was a successful woman who was extremely confident, decisive, and a good leader, though at times she could be abrasive. Deep down, Belle had a profound sense of unworthiness and struggled mightily with fear and doubt. The lie long ago turned into a secret she buried so deep within that she often felt out of kilter, a bit off balance.

She took a long, tough journey deep within to explore her need to be known. She desired the balance between being strong but not pushy, bold but not rude, and humble but not weak. Finding that balance would allow others to get to know her on a deeper, more authentic level.

Come along on this quest as Belle exposes the lie and finally uncovers a treasure within her through the power of forgiveness. With that gift will come tiny seeds of life that slowly sprout, changing her character and bringing love, joy, peace, and beauty.

## CHAPTER 1

# And The Walls Come A' Tumblin Down!

Belle stirred her perfectly brewed latte and slowly breathed in the serene surroundings. She sat at her favorite table in the cozy coffee shop's herb garden. The vine-covered trellis allowed just enough sunshine to peak through and brighten the garden while smells of cranberry scones wafted through the air.

She took out her journal and started writing out a plan of action. She knew exactly what she needed to do to accomplish the growth her company had forecasted. She began to write, and with each action item, she quickened the tapping her foot. She stopped to drink in the heavenly surroundings and smiled as she sipped her latte.

Within minutes, dark clouds began to roll in, threatening the perfect landscape. Strangely, one by one, things started to crumble around her. Large chunks of wood snapped off the trellis. The vine that covered it began to shrivel. The cobblestone patio disintegrated to dust, one brick at a time.

"What on earth is going on?" Belle said aloud as the people in the garden started to turn in their seats and look at her.

"How could you?" one woman said. "You're a horrible person," said a server who stopped to look at her. Belle struggled to remain calm and keep her composure. Large pieces of the building that she was sitting next to began to fall around her. The clouds burst with thunderous roars and bright flashes of light. The tables were turned over as though someone had been walking through the garden flipping them in the air, yet everyone was still in their seats, turned toward her, pointing and jeering. As Belle frantically stood to run for her life, she heard a voice cry, "Mom?"

Her heart stopped and then began to pound as she turned, hoping against hope for the moment she had waited for all these years.

## CHAPTER 2

## The Journey Begins

Belle threw back the covers and swung her legs around the side of the bed as she tried to catch her breath.

"Oh my God, that dream again!" She grabbed her cell to see the time. Almost three a.m. "How many times am I going to have that dream? What on earth could it possibly mean?" She looked at her phone again and scrolled through the long list of names. She landed on her therapist's name and began to type, "Can we meet today before you leave town?"

She put the phone down and shuffled to the bathroom, wiping the beads of sweat from her forehead. She gulped a glass of water and returned to bed. Concerned about falling asleep for fear of having the dream again, she knew if she didn't get more sleep, she would be worth nothing in the morning and her work would suffer.

Later that afternoon, Belle left her office early for the emergency therapy session. She referred to her therapist as her life coach, since everyone has a life coach these days. Heaven forbid anyone think she needed a therapist.

She walked into Sophie's office, appreciating the warmth she felt as she quietly closed the door. Her therapist was a sweet older woman who quietly nodded as Belle talked. *Thank God for Sophie,* she thought. *I'm not sure what I will do without her for two months while she's on her sabbatical.*

"Belle? Excuse me, Belle?"

## Danise C. DiStasi

"Sorry, Sophie. Where was I?"

"Well, you started to tell me about the dream, and I asked you if the dream is the exact same dream each time or if you can remember any differences."

"Oh, right—I was thinking. You know, I don't recall any differences. I think it is the very same dream."

Belle leaned back, closed her eyes, and took in a deep breath. Sophie smiled and nodded kindly.

"Belle, any idea why people are turning toward you accusing you of something?"

Belle sat straight up. "I have absolutely no idea. I am completely baffled and puzzled." Her eyes darted as she continued to think and then blew out a long sigh. "I don't know, Sophie. The whole thing confuses me. *Life* confuses me right now. I mean, here I am getting up in years. I feel like my life is in turmoil even though there's nothing wrong with my life, or so it seems. Maybe I should turn this marketing firm over to the next generation so I can retire and actually enjoy life." She stopped and picked a piece of lint off her sweater. "That's a problem, though—there is no next generation! Not anymore, that is!"

"And why is that, Belle?"

Belle gave Sophie a blank stare while wondering how many times she's going to have to go over these details. "Because my son is 2,000 miles away, and my daughter—well, you know. I haven't seen my daughter in years. I guess that makes me a failure as mother."

That unsettling feeling slowly stirred within Belle. *Maybe I should tell Sophie*, she thought to herself. *It's no big deal, not in today's world, anyway. Always a bit ahead of your time, Belle. Just leave it be.* She suppressed the feeling that she was being slowly sucked into a never-ending whirlwind.

"Sophie, what is the meaning of everything crumbling in my dream?"

# Hide And Seek

"When you are enjoying life or the surroundings in your dream, what are you doing?"

"I'm, uh, I'm doing just that—enjoying the surroundings!"

"And when the world starts crumbling, what are you doing?"

"I'm journaling!"

"Just journaling?"

"Well, no, I never 'just journal.' I'm journaling a plan."

"Think about that while we're on our break from one another. And one last question. What happens when you hear someone say, 'Mom'?"

Belle took in a deep breath. "My heart feels like it's going to burst. I turn to see who it is, and I wake up."

"Does the voice sound like that of your son or that of your daughter?"

Belle paused and started to say something, then shook her head. "My daughter."

Sophie nodded and smiled.

Belle swallowed hard and shook her head. "I miss her. I really, really miss her!"

Belle gave Sophie a warm hug. "I hope you have a safe trip, Sophie. I know you very much need this sabbatical, but," she shook her head, "I'm just not sure what I'm going to do without you."

"You know you can always call on Tom who is filling in for me, right?"

Belle waved her hand in the air to dismiss the suggestion, believing that no one could replace Sophie. The two hugged again and Belle turned to walk out of the office.

As she boarded the subway home, Belle went over the session with Sophie in her mind. She could not shake the troubling sense that something was bubbling up within her. She realized by this stage in her life that when that bubble-up feeling happens, a life lesson is about to erupt.

## Danise C. DiStasi

"What's the lesson this time, God?" She reluctantly asked, not expecting an answer, which was typical. However, this time she heard as though someone were standing right behind her. "Sometimes, Belle, the lesson isn't always about you."

"Great, just what I need: someone else's lesson invading *my* life!"

She smirked as she walked briskly through the subway car. She was strangely drawn toward a little girl sitting all by herself. She thought about walking past her but she immediately sat down next to her. "Do you mind if I sit here?" Belle asked. The little girl smiled and shook her head slowly as she watched Belle.

"Are you riding on this subway alone?" Belle asked. The little girl turned her head and looked out the window.

"Oh I see, how rude of me. You probably are not supposed to talk to strangers. No problem, but," Belle leaned closer to the little girl, "if you need help, just let me know."

Belle sat quietly and watched. She wondered why the little girl was alone as she observed the usual commuters in their private worlds, trying to be aware of others yet not wanting to be seen. She sank back in her seat and closed her eyes, trying to rest and push out the noise of the world around her, yet she felt that feeling stirring inside her.

She watched the little girl next to her sit quietly and patiently. She felt a familiar pang in her heart as she pondered, *What is the story with this child? Seems strange she would be on this route alone.*

She pondered this question and the questions Sophie had asked. She knew underneath her polished surface, she struggled with fear. Sophie did help her to at least acknowledge that. *But fear of what? What am I so afraid of?* If she were being honest with herself, she knew she had toughened up over the years. *But who wouldn't?*

Belle slowly stood to exit the subway. "Well, this is my stop. Will you be OK?" Belle asked the little girl. The little girl once again nodded, not saying a word.

# Hide And Seek

As Belle left the car, the little girl walked right behind her the whole time.

"Is this your stop too?" Belle asked.

The little girl nodded.

*Strange!* Belle thought and continued to walk, as did the little girl. "Should I be helping you?"

"I don't think so."

"Well, is someone here to meet you? Are you walking home alone?"

"No."

Belle rolled her eyes. *Great. Just what I need. Don't get involved, Belle!*

Belle continued to walk, occasionally turning to look for the little girl who had stopped quite a ways back and was standing alone. Her small silhouette seemed even smaller in the mist surrounding the streetlight. Belle slowly turned and kept walking, torn over whether to help the little girl or let it go. She decided she had to let it go. She couldn't help every needy person in this city.

She picked up her mail, unlocked the door to her home and flipped the switch to bring up a warm glow of lights. "Ah," she exclaimed as she kicked off her heels and placed the keys on the hallway table. She looked through one envelope after another and placed the pile on her kitchen table. She continued to think about the little girl.

"I just need to concentrate on something else," she said aloud. She thought about the counseling session and the questions Sophie asked.

Belle worked hard all her life to "prove herself" in the business world. And the business world applauded her toughness. But deep down she had a profound sense of unworthiness and struggled mightily with fear and doubt. She hid this by acting proud when in reality she didn't like who she had become and she didn't know how to change. Belle's bookshelves were filled with the latest business and self-help books. She read them cover-to-cover but rarely felt as though she was given a solution to her challenge of breaking through the fear and doubt.

Why was there a struggle now with this underlying fear? *Fear of what?* she asked again. *Am I afraid to lose my business? Am I afraid of being alone? What is this crazy fear thing?*

Belle poured a glass of red wine, started a fire and sat back in her favorite overstuffed chair as she pulled out her journal. A piece of paper torn from a book fell to the floor. On it was a highlighted section that read, "Every good and fruitful characteristic has a lie associated with it, and a clever mask that many hide behind because they struggle to justify the lie."

She leaned her head back and closed her eyes remembering why she placed the paper in her journal some time ago. She brushed a piece of hair out of her eye as she wiped away the painful memory of the last time she had seen her daughter, Jackie.

She wasn't sure if she had drifted to sleep or was imagining, but she heard a gentle whisper. "For a little while, I am going to ask you to shut down that voice that whispers negative thoughts of fear and doubt into your heart and mind. And yes, you have the power to shut them down, mighty strong woman. Rest as you begin this journey of seeing the masks you've let go of and others you've picked up. In that place of no distraction is the key to being open and willing to hear and see truth. It is possible."

## CHAPTER 3

---⚜---

# Love

Belle sat straight up in the chair realizing she had dozed off. The fire was a pile of dull embers, and her glass of wine was still half full. The sound of a text on her cell phone startled her. She grabbed her phone and peered through her glasses to see her assistant's name, Jann, appear at the top of the screen.

"Belle, I hope you had a great session with Sophie. Remember, you are profoundly loved!" She breathed in deeply to hold back any further emotion as she wiped her cheek. She typed quickly in response, "Thanks so much!" and then put the phone aside.

Belle wiped away another tear, not sure why it evoked such a pang in her heart. She prepared for what she hoped would be a good night's sleep, which she needed. She could not shake the image of the little girl standing alone while Belle walked further away from the subway stop.

The supplements hadn't worked at all for a much-needed good night's sleep. She tossed and turned, looked at her clock, looked at her phone until finally morning arrived. Belle set her phone in the speaker stand on the bathroom counter just in time to hear Tina Turner belting out "What's Love Got To Do With It?" She started a hot shower and rubbed her neck as the water warmed. She started humming and then mumbled, "Yeah, what's love got to do with it?" Like many executive women who survived the corporate world in the '80s and '90s, and still today, she pushed the L word so far back in the recesses of her mind.

# Danise C. DiStasi

She lingered an extra few minutes in the shower as she tried to relax in preparation for a very long day. Her career was her life now that her son, Todd, was married with three kids and lived on the west coast. Her daughter, Jackie, was—Belle breathed in slowly as she closed her eyes, dreaming of happier days gone by and hoping for a simpler, more relaxed life. A slight smile crossed her lips. "Oh, perhaps some day," she muttered aloud. She made sure she planned and prepared for that better day.

She finished her morning routine, made several calls, and as she locked the door behind her, she wondered if the little girl had made it to her destination.

The streets were bustling with activity. As she boarded the subway, she thought of how she was drawn to the little girl and how it seemed the little girl was drawn to her.

"Good morning, everyone!" Belle bellowed as she stepped through the sliding glass doors of her company. She often felt like this was Santa's workshop, with everyone bustling about, lots of energy and creativity. The marketing company was started by the Shippel family in 1972 as an agency built on the very same innovation and creativity she felt every morning when she walked through the door. Thanks to her and John, it was a global digital agency that combined traditional advertising and digital innovation. She had started as a receptionist and worked her way up. Several years later she and her husband had bought the company. After he passed away, she had taken on the role of CEO, much to the chagrin of the chairman of the board who had had his eye on that position when John was diagnosed with cancer.

"Good morning, Belle!"

"Hi Belle!"

"Morning, Ma'am!" came several salutations.

"Hi Jann!" Belle was always so happy to see her assistant, Jann. She was more of a dear friend than an assistant. Belle was not sure what she would do if Jann ever left her, but for now, she didn't want to think about it.

"Good morning, Belle! How was your evening?"

Belle cocked her head, not sure what to say about her evening. "Fine, thanks. Tossed and turned a bit, was really hoping for pretty decent night's sleep." She smiled as she stood by Jann's desk and looked at her. "Maybe I'll get that eight hours of sleep tonight. And thank you for the wonderful text. It was timely."

Jann smiled. "I was just thinking about you and all that you are going through."

"Thank you."

Jann handed Belle a cup of coffee as Belle walked into her office. "Agh!" Belle exclaimed as she jumped and dropped her coffee cup, struggling to catch her breath. There, not two feet away, was the little girl from the subway, smiling ever so sweetly and swinging her legs to and fro as she pertly sat in a leather chair.

Jann ran into the office, eyes wide, "Belle, are you OK?"

"What the—How did you get in here? Who—who are you?" Belle stammered.

Jann cocked her head to the side and then looked in the direction Belle was looking.

"How—how in the heck did you get in here?" Belle repeated.

Jann picked up the mug, "Belle? Are you talking to me or—who?"

Belle looked at Jann and then back to the little girl as she pointed toward the child. "Her!" Belle said as she continued to look in the opposite direction of Jann.

"She can't hear me or see me, Belle. Only you can see me," the child said sweetly.

Belle whispered, "What?" And then quickly turned toward Jann. "Oh, Jann, I am so sorry, I—I just remembered something. I was just thinking aloud." She feigned a smile and helped clean up the coffee. "I spilled a little coffee on me, which burned, and then that scared me, which made me drop my cup, blah, blah, blah. So sorry I scared you."

"Would you like another cup?"

"No, no, no. I just need to be alone, thanks. Oh, and can you shut the door? Thanks, Jann."

Belle's eyes pierced the little girl, who was not fazed by the activity or the desire on Belle's part to intimidate her.

"Alright. Enough games. Who are you?" she demanded.

The little girl's large brown eyes twinkled and her smile grew wide. She had adorable little dimples, and smooth, chestnut brown hair. "I'm you!"

Belle laughed nervously as she continued to look for any clues as to how this child entered her office. "What? Little girl," Belle said, firmly hoping to scare the child, "who are you? How did you get in here, and where are your parents?"

The little girl lowered her eyes and solemnly shook her head. "Well, my Mom passed almost twenty years ago."

"Huh?" Belle stopped cold and looked intently at the little girl. "Your mother could not have passed twenty years ago. You're barely— why you're barely five years old yourself," she gestured toward the child. "How could your mom have died twenty years ago?"

"Actually," said the young child as she scooted off the chair and toyed with a pen set, "I'm almost 6," she pulled her lip forward to show a gap in her smile, "and I'm losing teeth!" A sharp pang shot through Belle's heart as the words and gestures of the child reminded her of her own daughter. She shook her head as if to whisk away the memory lost so long ago.

Belle leaned against the edge of her desk, shaking her head. She stared at the child for several minutes and finally said softly, "Look, I am trying to help you. Can you help me do that?"

The little girl nodded.

## Hide And Seek

"I need to know who you are. What's your name? How did you get here, and how can I get you home as soon as possible?"

"And I am trying to help you," she said cheerfully, "Belle!"

Belle's eyes widened. "How do you know my name? Oh, I get it," she stood straight and began to frantically look around the office for any clue. "While I was talking with Jann, you found my cards and checked out my name." She stopped and looked at the little girl. "Can you even read?"

"Belle," the child said, oozing confidence, "I can do a lot of things, thanks to you!"

Belle sat down again and rubbed her forehead. "OK," Belle said aloud. "I'm losing it. That's the only explanation. Great time for Sophie to leave. I may need to set an appointment with her replacement, Tom. Geez, retirement needs to come much sooner than I originally planned. This is crazy." She held her fist in the air, as though she were angry with God, "What the heck is going on?"

The child stood, looking so sweetly at Belle, twisting side to side as though she were waiting for Belle to ask just one more question.

"At least tell me your name!"

"What name would you like me to have?"

"Seriously, child," Belle pursed her lips, "what name were you given? I know you have one, and you must know it since you're almost 6 years old."

"Belle."

Belle looked at her, waiting for her to continue.

"Belle is my name. You asked, 'What is your name?' and I'm telling you it's Belle."

Belle shook her head. "This is confusing—and ridiculous, I might add! I really need to not drink wine before I go to bed. It apparently has some strange lingering effects." She straightened up and her face beamed. "Oh . . . I get it. This is some sort of reality show where I get

## Danise C. DiStasi

to walk through life pouring wisdom into you—you know, like those questions of 'What would you say to the younger version of yourself?' right?"

The child smiled and tapped her chin, "Well, actually no!"

Belle's shoulders drooped as she held out her hands. "I give. What's going on?"

"I'm actually here to pour wisdom into you."

"That's impossible! You're a six-year-old child. What could I possibly learn from you? How on earth are you going to pour any wisdom into me?" said Belle, lips pursed in aggravation.

"Let's just see, shall we?"

Belle shook her head as she stood and walked to her desk. "This is just crazy! And what do I call you? Belle is confusing."

"Meme's good."

"Meme?"

"Yeah, you know, like 'mini me,' since I am a mini you. But Mini sounds like Mini Mouse, so let's just go with Meme, shall we?" The child giggled and held her hand to her mouth, her eyes twinkling! Belle could not help but smile.

"And," Belle sat down in her chair behind her desk and pulled out a mirror to make sure she didn't look as out of whack as she felt, "what am I supposed to do?"

"Well," said Meme with a smug look on her face, which then lit up as though she had just seen presents under a Christmas tree, "I know, let's pretend we're on an adventure of sorts, a real treasure hunt."

Belle raised her left eyebrow questioningly. "Great!" she said, dripping sarcasm. "And exactly how do we begin this little adventure?"

Meme leaned across the desk right above the mirror. Belle raised her eyes slightly and was surprised at the haunting resemblance. Meme smiled and said, "We've already begun. We're on the adventure of life together, me and you!"

## CHAPTER 4

# The Masks We Wear

Belle ran her finger under the edge of her lower eyelashes to remove a smudge and paused as she stared at her reflection. She noticed a few more lines around her eyes. They were slight, but there nonetheless. Meme stood by, watching, waiting.

"So, are you always going to be here? Just here?" Belle shrugged her shoulders and looked around. "I mean, do I need to feed you, take you home, do you want your own bedroom? I mean, how's this work?"

Meme smiled, shook her head side to side. "I'm not really sure either. It's sort of a journey for both of us. But I do know this: I seem most needed when you are most insecure."

Belle cocked her head to the side and peered at the little girl. "You're most needed when I'm most insecure? Soooo, you're saying I'm insecure now? Or is this a little intro howdy-do thing for us?"

Meme was silent.

"Hmm, that doesn't make much sense. I'm hardly insecure now. Jeesh, I've got tons of work to get to. What's so insecure about that?"

Meme—still silent.

"I can see this is going to be a lot of fun. Well," Belle turned to flip open her MacBook, "I've got work to do." She started typing away, hoping if she ignored the figment of her imagination, the little person would go away.

"What was the text about?"

Belle continued typing away as though she didn't hear her. Meme waited. As Belle hit send on an email, Meme settled into the big leather chair in the corner of the room and waited. "So, Belle, what was the text about last night?"

Belle shrugged, "Nothing. Just a friend trying to encourage me. She's sweet."

"Then why did it stir so much emotion?"

Belle stopped and looked at Meme. "Emotion? Hardly. I was just tired. There was no emotion there." She waved her hand as though swatting at a fly and yawned loudly. "So just make yourself comfortable and be a good girl, OK? And try not to talk." Belle went back to work.

Not a minute passed before Belle's eyes drifted toward the ceiling in thought. *Why did that text bother me so much? Jann was just trying to encourage me. She knows how things are for me sometimes. Why did it hit a nerve?*

A soft voice whispered from the other side of the office, "Was it because she expressed how much she cares for you?"

Belle whipped around in the chair. "OK, this is just creeping me out, talking to me like that in the middle of my thoughts." As Belle rose and paced back and forth, little Meme was curled up in the chair, same spot she was in when Belle turned her attention to her work. She was so small and so sweet Belle could hardly be upset.

"So what's the difference between you hearing a voice in your head or you hearing my voice? You listen to that little voice in your head all the time that feeds so much doubt, fear and even pride. What's the difference with me talking to you?"

"It's just creepy, that's all!" Belle brushed her hair out of her face and sat back down in her chair.

"Right! OK, and listening to the voice in your head is *not* creepy . . . hmm."

"That's different!" Belle looked at Meme and shook her head. "So what's the point? What are you trying to say to me?"

## Hide And Seek

As though invited to come closer, Meme jumped from the chair and knelt by Belle's feet, her big brown eyes looking up into Belle's face. "Belle, tell me why it is so difficult for you to think that a friend, much less a coworker, could truly care about you, about your life and struggles?"

"What do you mean? I don't have an issue with that."

"If anyone brings up the L word at work, you slam them. I'm just curious: why?"

"Well, clearly love doesn't belong in the workplace, right? Don't get me wrong: I love my kids, my family, the dogs I've had over the years." She looked up as though she were counting and shrugged, "and some friends. But I just think love should stay out of the workplace. It's—it's unproductive." She mumbled under her breath, "It should stay out of everything, for all I care."

Meme clasped her hands together. "Oh, why do we shy away from that word? Why does this one little four-letter word stir up such emotion for all of us? It can build an empire or topple the strongest leader. Perhaps someone said it to you and you didn't believe it?"

Belle gazed into Meme's eyes. *Is she for real? She's a kid and yet she seems so wise!*

"Are you asking me that?"

Meme nodded emphatically and said, "Yes! Or people who said they loved you were the very ones who hurt you. People rarely use *love* in the workplace, and when they do, they are told it is not appropriate or they are deemed too soft.

"But just as in your own life, underneath the polished surface, you and most people struggle with two major issues: (1) the fundamental desire to be deeply known and loved in spite of all our flaws and secrets, and (2) the struggle with a deep sense of unworthiness. Every human has a deep need to be known. But most women, because of their relational 'wiring,' are especially prone to desire people who are close to them to truly know and understand them. They desperately want to be known, yet that subtle sense of unworthiness—that they don't measure up—sabotages their well-being. Many successful, driven and hardworking women will tell you that they've never escaped the feeling of not being enough."

Belle sat in silence as though this young child had just pricked a hole in her heart and all the poison and junk she chose to believe poured out. *Does she know?* she asked herself. *Of course not—no one knows.*

Meme lowered her head as if she were disappointed in the entire human race. "It's so sad to me that people do not really understand love. They think they do when we feel all warm and snuggly with children or some boyfriend," she wagged her head back and forth as though she were Belle's mother scolding her for getting caught holding a boy's hand. "Like when you are attracted to someone and sense the butterflies. But really? Is that how people define and experience love, keeping it rooted in up and down feelings? With that understanding no wonder we tuck the word away and 'save' our energy for only big emotional experiences."

Belle slowly nodded her head, admitting that little Meme was correct. For many women, their emotions and feelings identify them, right or wrong. "Oh, she's such an emotional mess," or "She's so calm and cool all the time." For years, Belle was defined by her very strong personality.

"Am I right?" Meme raised her eyebrows and nodded.

Belle had to smile at her cute personality. "Well, yes, actually, you've hit the nail on the head."

"The fact is women are identified by a number of things other than who they truly are. Once they start walking in who they truly are and who they are created to be, they will no longer try to fit into the identity others have created for them. Most of us are living out a story that

## Hide And Seek

someone else wrote for us. And yet that is not at all who you were created to be."

Belle felt a familiar deep pang in her heart, a longing that she could not quite put her finger on. She snapped her head as if to shake herself out of a fog.

"If you feel like it is time to break out of that false identity and put down the fake mask," said Meme, "then let's get excited about this adventure together. It might be tough, but I think you can handle it." She winked. "Belle, let's finally break out of the crazy cycle of that mask we can call the 'unworthy mask.' You know the cycle: you want to be known, you don't feel worthy of letting people close, you gravitate to people who bring you down, and you withdraw more into yourself. The mask gets thicker and bigger."

"Yes, Meme, I'd love to. I'm just not sure how. And I am definitely not sure I would be the successful woman I am today had I not donned that mask. So letting go of it might be tough."

Meme stood slowly and walked to the bookcase. Her fingers scanned the many diverse books that Belle has read over the years. Finally she pulled one off the shelf. "Do you remember reading this?"

"Yes, I remember it well."

"In *Bold Love*, Dr. Dan Allender posed the question, 'At the core of your being do you believe God loves you?'"

Belle rolled her eyes and said, "Right! I remember putting the book down and honestly pondering that question. My first reaction was a resounding yes!"

Belle stopped and gave a far away look.

"Go on," said Meme.

"I remember thinking, *Really? Do I truly believe God loves me?*"

Meme gave a slight jump. "Exactly! Regardless of who people believe God to be or what role God plays in their life, everyone desires a connection to this greater being. It is innate in us, and we seek, or suppress, this connection from birth.

"Intellectually, we know the phrase, 'God loves you!' That conjures up sweetness and smiles. But remember the question you pondered in your heart at that time?"

"Yes," Belle whispered. "How weird, but yes, I remember like it was yesterday. I had to question whether I truly understood or believed that phrase. Did it pertain to me? If it did, how and why? The deeper question for me at that time was do I *trust* this love?"

"And what was your answer?"

Belle gave a nervous laugh. "A resounding no!"

"Ah," said Meme as though she were a professor with the final answer. "And therein was the issue right at the core of *your* being! How could you love others, and yourself, if you truly did not understand being loved at the deepest level of your being?"

Belle cocked her head to the side and thought about Meme's words. She shrugged, "Good question. I don't have an answer."

"Perhaps that is what we are supposed to unpack throughout our journey."

Belle was silent as she pondered the little girl who seemed to ooze wisdom. In the midst of her silence, Meme whispered, "Do you remember where you were when you read that book?"

Startled, Belle shook her head. "Um, no, I have no idea where I was. You mean physically, like was I sitting somewhere?"

Meme seemed to ignore the question. "It was about 15 years ago, and you and John had separated."

Belle gasped. *How does she know this?*

"I think it was a time when you were truly questioning love, remember? You wanted more, and he seemed happy with how things were. You needed more excitement, and, well, you were bored with him and your marriage."

# Hide And Seek

Belle remembered all too well. But since John's passing, she rarely thought of that time in her life, and she wasn't sure it was necessary to discuss it now.

"Well the reason I bring it up now, Belle, is that your obvious need for validation almost destroyed your marriage and family. You convinced yourself you were on the right track because you were happier and everyone commented on how good you looked."

Belle continued to stare at Meme as though she were going to challenge her but thought silence was best at this point. Her eyes stung as she held back tears. Finally she said, "We reconciled and worked it out. But you're right, I did question the whole notion of love."

"As most people do, Belle. Based on that experience, would you agree that the secret to a fulfilled life is receiving and giving unconditional love?"

Belle shook her head and then peered from the side at Meme. "I'm not sure I can actually agree with that right now, Meme."

Meme continued, "Most people, especially women, don't believe they are worthy of unconditional love. That's why so many women find themselves 'bored' after so many years of marriage."

"Go on."

Meme continued, "That causes people to walk in fear and believe the lie of rejection."

"Ouch!"

"And they hide behind the mask of pride to deal with the fear of rejection."

"Hmm. OK, Meme, let me see if I understand what you just said. The secret to a fulfilled life is receiving and giving unconditional love. Most of us don't believe we are worthy of unconditional love, which causes us to walk in fear and believe the lie of rejection..." Belle paused. "What exactly is the lie of rejection?"

Meme cocked her head to the side. "Rejection is always rooted in a lie. When we invite someone to an event and they don't accept, we

, or perhaps they don't like being with us. If someone doesn't respond to an email or text right away, we immediately think they are too busy for us, they have more important things to do than respond to us. You would never say those things to anyone, but you think them. And those thoughts are usually based on lies."

"Ahhhhh, so true! And when we think those things, at least for me, it stirs a lot of feelings. Depending on the situation, those could be very hurtful feelings. Oh, now I see—so we walk in fear and believe the lie of rejection and we hide behind the mask of pride to deal with the fear of rejection."

Meme's face beamed as she smiled, missing tooth and all. "Yep, that's it!"

"Let me think about this. But for now, I've got to get some work done."

"OK, Belle," Meme liltingly sang as she slowly seemed to fade away into the fabric of the overstuffed chair. An hour ago, watching that happened would have seemed preposterous, but now Belle just smiled and tried to concentrate on her work.

## CHAPTER 5

# What's Love Got To Do With It?

Jann gently placed a large glass of water and laid a pile of papers on Belle's desk. "I've been thinking of you. Thus the text I sent last night. Good thing. Mr. Hill called already this morning. He said it was urgent that you and he talk as soon as possible. He asked if you worked on the succession plan yet."

"Jeesh," Belle closed her eyes and leaned back against the seat. "Fine—call him and ask if we can meet in the morning. Perhaps bring some breakfast in, and he and I can talk about whatever's got him in such a tizzy these days."

"Will do," said Jann in her usual chipper voice.

Belle looked at Jann and said, "Jann, can I ask you a question?"

Jann shrugged her shoulders. "Sure!"

"Do you think using the word *love* is appropriate at work?"

Jann gave Belle a quizzical look and sat down in a seat across the desk from Belle. "What's going on? You don't usually ask me questions like that. Is everything OK?"

"Absolutely! I was just thinking about it last night. After I got your text, I thought about it." Belle smiled. "It was really sweet, and I appreciate your heart in wanting to reach out to me with an encouraging note. And it just made me think about that word *love*. And why don't we ever use it at work? Why do people bristle when someone in a work environment says that they love them?"

Jann looked at Belle for a long time. "That is a really great question, Belle. I know, I've often thought about that. You know me, I love giving hugs and letting folks know I care about them. I'm not sure I have an answer, but maybe this story about my dog might be a way to think of love in the workplace."

"Your dog?" Belle looked over her glasses and raised her eyebrows.

Jann laughed and smiled widely. "I know, seems crazy, but humor me. Do you have time for me to tell the story?"

Belle nodded, resigned to listen no matter how silly.

"I adopted a dog several years ago. I had decided not to have any more pets, but when I encountered this abandoned mutt with big brown eyes and a sweet temperament, I knew I had to adopt her. I soon discovered that Lily brought a lot of emotional baggage to our relationship. She demonstrated behaviors that concerned me, and I immediately engaged a dog trainer. I quickly realized I needed training as much as Lily did, if not more so."

"Hmm," muttered Belle. "Go on."

"I had to provide excellent leadership skills to train that crazy dog, which took work, time, and discipline. And," she said emphatically, "that training had to be rooted in love. Lily needed so much love, and that wasn't easy due to some of her rough edges. When I chose to adopt her, I chose to deal with whatever baggage came with her. I knew I would need to press through issues she might not want to deal with."

Belle took a sip of water. "Interesting comparison. Keep going."

"The kind of love Lily needed, the kind any one you come in contact with needs, was patient and kind. Belle, I am absolutely convinced it takes strength and courage to love. Some people would attest that loving dogs is much easier than loving people. It is more than being nice to someone; it's about letting go of your stuff and serving another.

## Hide And Seek

"Lily was deeply loved. She was not perfect, but for the first time in her life she was loved. And what a huge change there has been in that dog. Love is the very foundation of our relationships, and trust is a building block. Trust is not automatic, yet without it, there is little chance of building a deep relationship."

Jann sat forward in her chair and passionately said, "Imagine, Belle, if we could harness that kind of power and energy in the workforce just because of love," she beamed. "What a difference it would make!"

Belle slowly nodded her head as she carefully thought about the words that were said.

Jann stood up. "I'm not sure if I answered your question, but I for one am all for talking about genuine love in the workplace."

Belle nodded, feeling as though she were in slow motion. "Good point, Jann! You're a wise young lady. Thanks. I will give that some thought."

Jann walked out of Belle's office and closed the door behind her. Belle started to sift through the papers on her desk.

"Really good points," came a voice from the "living room" area of the office, which startled Belle as several papers landed on the floor.

"Oh my God, could you please not enter my life like that?"

"Like what?" asked Meme with a giggle as she jumped off the large leather couch and started toying with the knickknacks on the shelf. She straightened a family picture that Belle kept on the bookshelf.

"Where you just appear!"

"I've been here the whole time," Meme smiled. All four of her front teeth were missing. "I liked what your friend said about love. Makes sense, right?"

Belle shook her head side to side, "I have no idea what to think. But I am really busy right now, and I don't want to have to explain why I have a kid in my office that just appears out of nowhere."

"Mind if I chime in on what Jann said?"

Belle sighed, rolled her eyes and pushed the papers back on her desk. "Do I have a choice?"

Meme was silent as the rustling of the papers stopped and Belle looked directly at Meme. She leaned back in her chair and folded her arms. "Ok. Go ahead."

Meme gently smiled. "I personally think that loving others means we want to serve someone joyfully for *their* good, not because we were looking for something in return."

Belle shrugged. "Ok!"

"Belle, look at what true, deep love really means. If you look at it as something to 'get' from others, you will be miserable and unsatisfied. If you believe you don't need it, you will be unfulfilled. If you are operating out of fear, which leads to self-protection resulting in the harm of others, love will always be elusive, and you will be hurt easily by others' actions."

Silence.

Meme continued, "If you show affection to others for selfish reasons based on deep wounds, hurtful pasts and simply as a way of self-medicating, you will find yourself attracted to others for how they make *you* feel. You will be that 'nice, sweet person' people say phony, flattering things about. Nothing wrong with being nice and sweet, but if it is to receive accolades to make yourself feel better, you will be miserable, and nothing will ever be good enough for you."

"Child, your wisdom blows me away!"

Meme giggled, and then got very serious. "The good news is we *do* have a choice! Belle, do you choose to believe you are deeply loved?"

Belle stared at Meme, not moving or breathing. Finally she let out a breath. "I am desperately trying to believe that."

An instant message from Jann popped up on Belle's screen: "Mr. Hill will be here at 7:00 a.m. tomorrow. Chef will have a piping-hot breakfast for you both."

## Hide And Seek

Meme reached out to touch Belle's hand but stopped short as she noticed Belle glance quickly at her hand. She slowly pulled back and gave Belle a warm smile. "Perhaps the best place to start is with Mr. Hill."

Belle smirked and shook her head. She could not imagine ever loving Alex Hill.

CHAPTER 6

# No Love, No Way

5:00 a.m. came much quicker than Belle wanted it to. She opened her eyes and already a wave of anxiety flooded her thoughts.

"Gooooooooood morning, Miss Belle," came a chipper voice right in Belle's ear. Belle turned to the side and found herself nose to nose with Meme.

"Really, Meme," said a very sleepy Belle, "I'm not much of a morning person. Can you just tone it down, please?"

Meme continued to look into Belle's face but remained silent. Then, as if she could not help herself any longer, she gently whispered, "This is going to be a great day!"

Belle rolled over and remembered she had an early breakfast with Alex. She groaned aloud at the thought as she stretched and went through her morning routine, Meme at her side the entire time.

She walked into the office an hour earlier than most folks arrived and was taken by the quietness and serene sense of purpose. She missed the days many years ago where she used to get into the office much earlier than everyone else and the quietness helped her ease into her day.

As she walked through the quiet halls, she looked to her side and found Meme intently walking with her, brows furrowed as though she were deep in thought.

"Why, Meme," Belle chided, "you seem worried about this meeting. Should I be concerned?"

## Hide And Seek

Meme's face suddenly perked up, and a smile spread across her cherub face. "I'm not sure, Belle."

That did concern Belle. She was beginning to rely on Meme's mood and wisdom to set the tone for whatever might come. She felt like she was on her own in this situation. But she was used to that as she's had to take control of many situations in her life.

Alex Hill had been a nemesis from the beginning for Belle. She was not looking forward to her breakfast with him. She knew exactly what he wanted.

Belle and Alex went way back, long before she even met her husband, John. Alex had been the star of the football team. They dated, and everyone thought they were destined to marry. However, things didn't work out, and then she met John. She immediately fell in love and never looked back. It just so happened that Alex and John were friends from childhood. And her husband always loved Alex. But Alex was not the trusting friend that her husband thought he was. Nonetheless, John was fond of Alex and remained loyal to him throughout his entire life.

"Good morning, Alex!" said Belle as soon as she walked into the waiting area outside her office. Alex was pacing, looking out the large glass windows overlooking the city. He turned and politely kissed her on the cheek, saying, "Good morning, my dear! How are you?"

"I'm actually well, thank you," said Belle as she turned to give a sideways glance to Meme who was still by her side, apparently invisible to Alex. "Please," Belle pointed towards the table, "have a seat. Our breakfast should be here momentarily."

As they took their seats, Belle said, "Alex, I know exactly why you're here, so let's just get right down to business."

Alex raised his eyebrows. "Of course. Belle, it has been—what, four years or so since John passed away. While the company is doing OK, it could be doing so much better. I know you're a fabulous leader. I'm just not quite sure you are *the* leader to lead the ship in the direction it needs to go. I, of course, want to make sure that I adhere to the promise I made to your husband that you would be well taken care of."

Belle stood as the breakfast was rolled in on a cart. She walked over to the credenza, went through a stack of papers, and pulled out a sheet. As the breakfast was placed in front of them, Belle looked over the sheet of paper and then at Meme, who was sitting on the couch with her little arms folded, sweetly smiling. Something was different about Meme's smile. She seemed to exude confidence. Belle wasn't quite sure she could put her finger on it, but she couldn't linger looking at Meme for fear Alex would think she was crazy.

"Alex," Belle said, "I really appreciate your concern. And I can't say I disagree with you, because I do believe we're just at a plateau right now. Personally, I know we are on a trajectory that will definitely get us out of this plateau and into a steady, sustainable growth. Alex, I know you want to be CEO, right? You do know that if you take over as CEO, including my shares in the company, we will no longer be a woman-owned business. Many of our large clients depend on our WBE status for their diversity spend. We won't be able to offer that benefit any longer if you own the majority of this business which could put us at risk of losing our largest clients."

Alex rolled his eyes and put his hands up in the air. "What difference does that make, Belle? Does that actually generate any business for us?"

Belle placed in front of him a sheet of paper that showed the statistics on the business they had brought in due to their WBE status.

Sensing his disinterest, she looked him straight in the eyes and said, "Alex, why is taking over my business so important to you?"

Alex looked very surprised. "I owe it to my friend."

"He was my husband. Do you think I don't owe this to him myself?"

"Belle, I'm not sure you are capable of doing it. Please understand, I think you are a wonderful woman, a fabulous leader, a great mom, and you've been a wonderful wife to my friend. But as CEO of a company, Belle, it is clear you do not have the experience needed to run a company."

"And why do you think I'm not capable of doing this? Or that you are even more capable?"

He looked at her from under his eyebrows, cocked his head to the side, and said, "Belle, I have experience in turnarounds, in building businesses, and salvaging horrible ones." He raised his brow and said, "Not to toot my own horn but with the three companies I currently own, I've made sure I have scalability built into our operations. It's not just about market share. I've clearly established goals and objectives needed in order to deliver service and product efficiently over long periods of time—and it obviously works." He leaned forward and sternly looked at Belle. "You do not have the same capabilities."

Belle forcefully leaned forward. "That's the reason for the Board, Alex, and why John and I poured so many years into developing our incredible executive team. It takes a team, not one man. That's why we invested in Chuck, our CFO and Lynne, our COO. It's a team. You clearly have forgotten about the people factor, Alex." She hesitated, knowing her voice was getting louder. "We have built this company from the ground up. What makes you think I cannot run it successfully?" Belle peered at Alex. "Is there something else going on, Alex? Is this really just about this business?"

Alex leaned back, took a deep breath, and closed his eyes. "I was hoping it would not have to come to this, Belle, but I may have to ask the board to remove you."

Belle's mouth dropped open as she took a breath. "What?" She asked slowly. So not to let him see her give any stronger reaction she stood to walk behind her desk. While deep inside Belle expected those words to come out of his mouth, when they did they stung. "Alex, do what you feel you have to do. But at this point, I am keeping my company, I am keeping it for John's sake, and I am going to work my tail off to make sure it's successful, even if that is in spite of you. Now, if you'll excuse me, I have work to do."

Alex stayed seated and looked at her. Belle looked back at him, lowered her eyes and said, "Do you think it would honor my husband if he heard us talking to one another like this?"

"I have absolutely no doubt it would not honor him," said Alex in a whisper.

"I know," said Belle. "Why don't you give me one year to get this company off the plateau and moving in the upward trend that we have experienced over the years."

Alex cocked his head to the side and then leaned forward on one elbow. "What makes you think you can do it in one year?"

Belle glanced over at Meme, then back at Alex and said, "I'm not quite sure I can tell you at this point, Alex, but I just know in my heart something has changed, and everyone's going to benefit from it."

Belle walked to the door and opened it. "I hope you have a really good day today, Alex." Alex put on his trench coat as he walked toward the door. He stopped, looked at the floor and then leaned closer to Belle. "I'll recommend to the board that we look for your replacement. You'll have until the end of the next quarter."

"You don't have a right to do that, Alex. Don't put your make believe time pressures on me."

"I am merely making a suggestion to the board, Belle, that's all. If you are all that you say you are, then that time frame should not be a problem." And with that, Alex walked out. Neither said goodbye.

Belle gently closed the door and breathed out slowly. She looked at Meme, who looked very serious. "So, that went well," said Meme, softly.

Belle walked swiftly to her desk. "Who does he think he is? Five months?" She started moving papers around. "Who cares? We're on track, and we'll continue on the path of growth."

## Hide And Seek

"Well, then what are you upset with? Sounds like you have it handled."

"It ticks me off that he thinks he can give me an ultimatum. No problem! I've got this."

Meme sat back in the chair with her palms facing each other and the fingertips touching as she whistled. Belle stopped shuffling papers and looked at Meme. "What?" Belle said sharply.

"Do you remember our talk yesterday about love? How would that conversation have gone if you truly loved that man?"

Belle shook her head slowly and narrowed her eyes. "Meme, I don't have time to do your warm fuzzy stuff. I'm in a battle right now, and the discussion about love just walked out the door with Alex."

Meme slowly nodded and said softly, "I see. We'll have to revisit this subject another time." Belle went back to her paperwork. Just then her phone buzzed with a text message. As she read the message, her furrowed brow softened. Her eyes brimmed with tears, and she held her hand to her mouth as she whispered, "Oh my God!"

She looked at Meme, whose usual perky expression was now grave. Belle grabbed her coat and bag and as she ran out the door. When she looked back, Meme was gone.

CHAPTER 7

# Joy In The Moment

Belle rushed past the information desk, knowing exactly what room she needed to go to. She frantically pressed the elevator's call button and hit number 11 when she got on. She slowly took in a deep breath and noticed the elevator's other occupants: a young lady with a mask over her mouth and nose and a gleaming bald head with a smile penned on its left side; a woman Belle assumed was the child's mother, standing next to her child and rubbing the back of her neck; a nurse who was reading her phone; and a young woman who stared at the numbers clicking away. The only person who showed any emotion was the child, whose eyes seemed to beam with life.

*How strange*, Belle thought to herself, *that the one person who is gravely ill is the one with so much life!*

She finally came to the room. Number 1117. The room she had visited many times over the last several months. She stopped, hesitant to go in, afraid of what she might see. As she stepped in, the room was strangely quiet. The bed was empty, as was the room. Belle hung her head and started to weep. Just then she felt a hand on her heaving shoulder. As she looked up, her friend, who had just stepped out of the bathroom and was wiping her hands, smiled and hugged Belle.

"Oh, Belle, thank you so much for coming."

Belle wept into the woman's shoulder. "Lisa, I am so sorry. I'm sorry I wasn't here this week. I'm sorry all this happened. I'm—"

## Hide And Seek

"Belle," Lisa softly pushed Belle to where she could look into her face. "No worries, honest! This is as good a time as any to be here with me. Maybe even better. Max went to take care of some things, and I am packing what I need to."

Belle seemed confused. "Your text? You said that Carly went home. I am assuming home to—"

"Yes, she went home. Heaven home, with the Lord."

Belle held her mouth and shook her head. "How? Why? And how are you doing?"

"Belle, I've known for a long time my child was going to die. We were given one year with her, and she lived two and a half years, a year and a half longer than they predicted. *That* is a downright miracle, right? We've been in these last stages in this room for, oh let's see, five weeks?"

"Where is—where is she?"

"They took her body to the morgue. But she's in heaven with Jesus."

The two friends sat down together on the small couch in silence. Nurses were in and out, moving hospital equipment, preparing the room for the next patient.

"I'm sorry Lisa. I know we've been preparing, but I am still in shock. Loosing a seventeen-year-old child—it's unthinkable. I am so sorry for your pain!"

Lisa nodded. "I only wish I knew. . . ."

"Knew what?" Belle asked.

"What was that moment like for her? That very moment when Carly left her worn-out little body that was so racked with pain and horrible cancer." Lisa looked directly at Belle and smiled. "Can you imagine, Belle?" Her eyes brightened. She looked up as though she was able to see through the building to a celestial place. Almost breathless, she went on. "Imagine! She hadn't been able to walk for the last three months at least, and since the diagnosis—well, we tried to keep life normal, but how do you do that with chemo and surgery and hospice and—well, you know all that." Lisa stood up. "The freedom I felt for her the minute she breathed her last breath—Belle, I knew then she was free. And while I sobbed in poor Max's arms for what seemed forever, I could only feel joy, joy that my baby was finally free from that horrendous disease."

Belle was stunned, but Lisa turned quickly on her heels and said, "Let's go down to the coffee shop and get a cappuccino. I really do need to get away from this room. It just reminds me of, well, of death, and right now Belle, I want to think of life. Do you mind?"

Belle shook her head. "No, not at all! Are you sure you're up to it?"

"This is a hospital, Belle! They're used to people crying in their coffee shop. I'm good. If I need to cry, I'll cry. And you're OK with that, right?" The two friends laughed, a stark contrast to the surrounding sense of death that lingered in the room. "Max is taking care of some paperwork, and I will meet up with him in about 30 minutes. Time with you will do me good."

Lisa and Belle walked arm in arm down the hall to the elevator. Lisa was a young up-and-coming executive whom Belle had met several years ago. While Belle was a business mentor of Lisa's for years, the tables seemed to turn when Lisa's daughter, Carly, started complaining of headaches and blurred vision. She was quickly diagnosed with an inoperable brain tumor and given shockingly little time to live. From that point on, Lisa was the teacher and Belle drank in every bit of wisdom she could glean. Lisa's deepening faith stood in stark contrast to that of Belle, who felt as though she were watching a movie of a true hero, someone she could only wish to be. But Belle had little interest in any discussion of faith, so the topic was rarely broached.

Lisa wrapped her hands around a warm cup of pumpkin spice cappuccino as she looked out the window of the small hospital coffee shop. She smiled and looked back at Belle. "This was Carly's favorite time of year, the start of the holidays. Thanksgiving was just a blur this year, but we managed to get in some fun things for her. One of her favorites was drinking yummy chocolate or coffee drinks like this," she said as she sipped the hot beverage, leaving a slight white mark on the tip of her nose. She laughed as she wiped it off.

Belle slowly shook her head. "Lisa, I have to tell you, I am amazed at your composure and strength. Are you sure you're OK? I mean, I just don't want you to come crashing down when no one is around because they all think you're 'OK.'"

Lisa leaned forward. "Belle, no, I am not OK. My beautiful daughter has died. She will never cheer at another football game. She won't go to her senior prom. She won't get married and have children. Losing her will forever cast a shadow on everything I do, everything we do, because she's not here and never, ever will be again. I can't pretend that is OK with me. It's not," Lisa said emphatically as she sat back in her chair. Belle nodded her head, listening intently.

"I've had incredible mood swings, being filled with joy, celebrating my baby's life and then mad as hell at God. How could he let this happen? Asking why over and over again. The next few weeks will be absolutely miserable as I try to get back into life. Oh, Belle, the pain that just rips through my heart is intense. I feel like someone is just shredding my heart to pieces." Lisa started to weep. Belle reached across the table and touched her arm.

"But," Lisa said, dabbing her eyes with a tissue, "at the same time I cannot explain this deep welling-up feeling of inexplicable joy!" She shook her head, her eyes lit up as she sat up straighter and her whole countenance changed. "I sometimes feel like I must have a split personality: up one minute, down the next. But this morning as I was kissing Carly's precious face, I knew in my heart that she hadn't had a choice whether to live or die. But I do. If I want her life to mean anything, I have to choose to continue on, to live in honor of her and God and to choose joy!" She let out a sigh, and with eyes full of life and tears, she looked at Belle and said, "Belle, I choose life." She shrugged her shoulders. "I choose life! Not only that, I choose a joy-filled life." She looked out the window again as Belle looked with wonder at her dear, sweet friend whose face seemed to glow with joy.

Belle sat quietly as she watched her friend drink in the memories of autumns past. Finally, Lisa took in a long, slow breath. "You know, Belle, in our world today, we are enthralled with the word *happy*. Companies have policies in place to be a happy work environment. When things are bad, we go to our happy place to help us survive. We take happy pills. We let people know when we are feeling happy and when we're not so happy. We put on our happy face." She took a sip of coffee. "But I bet most of us never have to let anyone know how we're feeling because it is always obvious in our behavior. But happiness is not the same as joy. Happiness is very dependent on our feelings."

"I totally agree, but I have to ask, what is so bad about that?"

"I would ask that very same question. I mean, after all, being happy is a good thing, right?" Belle nodded. "Sure it is, if you like the ups and downs of mood swings and that internal talk that goes on in our heads, trying to convince us we're OK, everything is OK.

"We've all been around folks who swing high, then low, then high. Now, I'm not talking about people who have a serious medical issue with moods or depression. I'm talking about people who are emotionally stable yet teeter every day on what sort of mood they are in. We're never quite sure which moods we will be dealing with, so we hold back in our connection with them until we observe which personality shows up.

"I've worked under people like this. On good days, when the boss is happy, everyone is in a good mood. But if the boss is in a lousy mood, we stay in our offices and keep our heads low. And we lie. When it comes time to fill out the cultural information, we check the box that

## Hide And Seek

says we work in a happy place. No one dares to upset the apple cart." Belle swallowed hard, wondering if she was that kind of boss.

Lisa moved her water glass toward the server, who asked if she needed more. "Sure, thank you!" She was clearly formulating a thought, and Belle was happy to let her work on it. "You know Belle, we post pictures of our perfect life, how happy we are, how getting a promotion makes us happy, how our spouses make us happy. Oh, it breaks my heart to see that most of us wear masks with a smile plastered on our faces. We smile in our professional pictures and yet complain about how much we hate our jobs.

"Personally, I think women are especially prone to this because we are deeply emotional beings. We love feelings and rely on them intuitively to connect with others. Sadly, some have used this to exclude women leaders. But I think our barometer of feelings is what makes us uniquely gifted to be incredible leaders. And we can be incredible leaders who are filled with deep, meaningful joy when we go deeper than the surface of our emotions. We have the power to do that.

"I would never ask to experience what we did these last couple of years, but I have learned a very valuable lesson—not one I care to learn ever again, once is enough for me, thank you, Jesus. I get it! I believe we can truly experience joy—deep, unwavering, resounding joy—no matter the circumstances. And every human being is capable of experiencing this. We are designed as women to exude love and be wrapped in pure joy. But it will take a special peeling away of the superficial layer we tend to hide behind. Belle, I am done hiding behind a mask that the business world, or our society itself, insists we wear. While I would never want to experience what we've gone through over the last two years, I've experienced more life and joy than I have in my entire life."

Belle stared at her friend in amazement. She could not even imagine the word *joy* being in any sentence about what Lisa had experienced.

"Truth!" said Lisa. "I have learned that joy is an important *practice*, and I believe that comes from gratitude, hope, and love. It is the pure and simple delight in being alive," her eyes lit up, "and being thankful for our lives. Joy is our elated response to experiences of life, even when life is tough. It is our response and deep satisfaction when we are able to serve others, not as an obligation but because our heart prompts us to do so."

Belle shook her head slowly. "But how could watching your beautiful daughter waste away with a horrible disease *ever* bring joy?"

"Because I believe, and Carly did too, that joy is delighting in the beauty of something beyond ourselves, even in difficult times of loss, disappointment, and pain. The talks she and I had, nose to nose because she was so weak, were some of the best discussions I could ever imagine. It was as though she were witnessing the very outskirts of heaven, and wisdom exuded from that precious baby."

Belle reflected on her words. She had been around people who exuded a sense of calmness and peace no matter what they might be going through. But this was beyond her comprehension. *How could she possibly stay so strong? Something's got to give.* Belle noticed Meme sitting on a stool, hands in her pocket as she intently watched the two friends converse. Belle had expected her to show up.

"I know," Lisa tipped her head to the side. "It sounds crazy, I get that. Trust me, I've had every self-talk and doubt flood my brain and heart, and it's almost impossible to stop." She dabbed her eyes. "That damn self-talk tears at the fiber of my being and rips apart any sense of peace. I am so good at allowing it to creep in. And guess who is right behind it? Fear and doubt! Jeesh!" She blew her nose.

Belle was happy to let her friend process the swirling emotions, but she could not help but think the words were not just the empty stirrings of a grieving mom. Belle took out her notebook to jot a note.

## Hide And Seek

Lisa was used to her friend jotting notes, so she continued. "Don't you just hate fear and doubt? They come in, completely take control of our emotions, and then control our behaviors. Behavior controlled by fear and doubt is always destructive. I've seen it, and you have too!" Belle nodded her head as she wrote the words *fear* and *doubt* and then the name *Alex Hill*.

"I prefer to live with joy," said Lisa, "because I like the deep down sense that all is well. Even in the midst of what I experienced. I love the bubbling-over feeling within us that says there's hope." She started to cry and wiped her tears. "Tough as it was, I came to understand that hope does not lie in the better life here. Hope was not that Carly would be miraculously healed and get up and walk out of this hospital. Oh how I so desperately wanted to see that, down to the very last minute. But I trusted in a hope that was beyond my own understanding and comprehension. I cared more for my precious Carly, for her freedom from pain, burdens and struggles. There, in that very thin, teetering space is where I found true, deeply resounding joy. And that joy propelled me to take just the very next step, small as it may have been."

Lisa shook her head. "It seemed so preposterous that I had to actually journal the times when I sensed true, deep, meaningful joy. I knew I would slink into anger and desperate grief, so I wanted to capture those moments and reflect on the genuine sense of excitement that there is more to life than hoping to be happy. An overwhelming sense of peace billows over me like a warm blanket on a brisk winter morning when I remember those moments with Carly."

Lisa reached across the table and held Belle's hands in hers. "Belle, I want to practice joy! For Carly's sake, that her life meant something and will continue to mean something, I believe there is hope. It is the pure and simple delight in being alive, and I am thankful for her life and ours. We had a certain time with her, and, believe it or not, we knew when that time would end." She dropped her head and started to cry. "My heart breaks for the moms who can't have that final goodbye because their child was in an accident or, worse, took their own life." She breathed in deeply as though she were not able to bear thinking how awful that pain must be. "But I had that precious time, tough as it was. We had our time together. And so when life gets tough—and nothing could be tougher than what Max and I experienced—I've made a decision to choose joy!"

Belle smiled and squeezed Lisa's hands. "You amaze me, my friend. Oh, I wish that I could be as strong as you."

"Well, buck up, sister, because I am going to need your strength over the next, oh, rest of my life!"

The two friends laughed as they stood to leave the café. Meme jumped off the chair with a lilting movement and came alongside Belle. Belle resisted the urge to hug her as she would her own child, knowing it might look like hugging air.

As they walked out, Max met them back at the room, and they all hugged together for a long time. A nurse interrupted with the final papers just as Belle's cell phone vibrated in her pocket. Not recognizing the number, she motioned to her friends if it was OK that she answer. They nodded as they turned their attention to the nurse, and Belle answered, "Hello, this is Belle."

"Mom?" Belle stopped, her eyes widened as she listened to the voice again say, "Mom, it's me. Ya there?"

## CHAPTER 8

# Peace And Forgiveness

Belle could hardly believe her ears. The sound of her daughter's sweet voice melted Belle's heart. Belle looked at Meme, who looked surprised as well. Lisa and Max were in the throes of finalizing paperwork. Max had his arm around Lisa's shoulder as she dabbed her eyes.

"Well, hi honey!" Belle stammered. "Is everything OK?"

"Yeah, just wanted to say hello."

"Oh, I'm so glad." Belle walked to the end of the hall to a little sitting area. She gave Max and Lisa space to take care of the things they needed to while she talked with her daughter on the phone. She didn't even realize Meme walked close beside her.

"So what's going on? Is everything OK?" Belle asked again, not sure what to say.

"Mom, everything is fine." There was a long pause as Belle looked out the large window at the end of the hall, experiencing absolute joy that she heard her daughter's voice and then concern that something may be wrong. Meme took a seat and watched her. Her daughter, Jackie, continued. "It's been awhile—"

"Three years, two months, and five days, but who's counting," Belle softly smiled, but the silence on the other end of the phone sliced through any levity. Belle resisted the urge to share about Carly's passing in hopes that maybe that would spur her daughter on to reconcile. Though Belle and her daughter had the typical mother-daughter issues,

## Danise C. DiStasi

Belle was never really sure why her daughter had stopped talking to her. After Belle's husband died, Jackie left and made no attempt to reconnect. Meme was sitting on the edge of the couch, slowly shaking her head side to side as if to say, "Just listen."

Jackie sighed, "Mom, I know. Trust me, things have been weighing heavily on me lately. I don't want to have a big long discussion or argument. I just need to share some things with you."

"OK," Belle said softly. And listen she did.

"Mom, I'm so sorry," she started to cry. "I just wanted to live away from your shadow, out from under your big," she hesitated, "your big, I don't know, your whatever it is that you are."

Belle listened.

"I just needed air. I felt like I was choking there. Your expectations of me—the business—dad dying, it was all too much! Then as time went on, it just seemed like I couldn't call or reach out, so I stuffed it, hoping it would all just go away."

"Oh, honey," Belle started, but Meme shook her head side to side again. Belle remained quiet but could hear soft sobs from her daughter. It was killing her not to reach out to her.

"I've had a lot of time to think about things, and I just wanted to call and say I am sorry. Will you forgive me?"

"Of course I forgive you, oh Jackie, of course. Will you forgive me for being that overbearing mom and not appreciating who you are? You are an—"

Meme was gesturing her to be silent. Belle immediately got it. She knew she was doing the "I'll trump *your* apology with mine," and she stopped. "Jackie, yes I forgive you. Thank you for asking." She could still hearing soft crying.

"Mom, I am not sure what this all means, and I'm not willing to throw everything to the wind, but maybe we can talk another time."

"Sure, sure," she turned and saw Max and Lisa putting on their coats, causing Belle a pain in her heart at the finality of it all. "Honey, can we talk soon? I would love to talk for hours with you."

Jackie interrupted. "I know, I know. You're busy, I knew I was taking a risk calling you in the middle of the day."

"Well, actually, I'm not at work. I'm at a hospital with Lisa and Max." Lisa and Max had been in Belle's life for a long time and Jackie knew them well. "Carly was diagnosed with an inoperable brain tumor about two years ago." She heard Jackie gasp. Belle bit her lip and breathed deeply. "Carly passed just a few hours ago," Belle said softly.

Silence.

"Oh, my God, I had no idea!" Her crying was much more prominent. "Poor Lisa and Max, I am so sorry. This is awful, just awful."

Belle teared up as well and nodded but had no words to share.

"Will you let me know what the funeral arrangements are?"

"Yes, honey, I sure will. Is this your cell number you called me from?"

"Yes."

"Jackie, it was good to hear from you. Thank you for calling me. While I would love to talk with you every minute, every day, you decide when you want to talk again. Is that OK with you?"

"Sure, Mom, that'll work. But will you call me with the arrangements for Carly?"

"Yes. I love you honey!"

"Thanks, Mom, we'll talk soon!"

Belle hit the end call button and turned to see Max and Lisa walking toward her. She gave them both a hug. As they weaved their way through the all-too-familiar hallways of the hospital, they exchanged details about the next steps, walked out into the brisk air, and said their goodbyes. As Belle stood waiting for a cab, Meme slowly slipped her small hand into Belle's hand. Just slightly above a whisper, Meme said, "Strange that today your friend loses her daughter while yours came back."

Belle stared ahead as though she didn't hear Meme. She held Meme's hand loosely, realizing it was the first time they had actually touched. Belle's eyes widened, still not sure who or what Meme is, but somehow her presence always offered a sense of peace. She glanced at Meme, who seemed a bit taller. Belle smiled, her heart ready to burst from the range of emotions she felt today; anger toward Alex, confusion about Meme, unspeakable sadness about Carly, and overwhelming joy in hearing Jackie's voice. Yet in the midst of these various emotions, an overwhelming sense of peace flowed over her. "Yes, very strange indeed."

## CHAPTER 9

# Ah, Elusive Peace

Belle explained to Jann all that had taken place. "And could you hold all my calls? I just need time to think right now."

"Sure! By the way, we have pizza in the back. Would you like a couple of slices?" said Jann as she organized a stack of papers on Belle's desk.

"Oh, that'd be great, thanks."

Belle settled into the couch as Jann placed the plate of pizza on the table and then quietly closed the door. Belle took her shoes off and rested her feet on the ottoman with a long slow sigh. Meme stood next to the couch, her head tilted with a very serene look on her face that depicted exactly how Belle felt. *Peace* was all Belle could think. In the midst of chaos, just peace.

"Oh, just the mere sound of that word, *peace* rolling off our tongues is ever so soothing and calm." Belle was getting used to Meme being so profound and almost reading her mind. She reveled in the sense of peace and smiled, then took a bite of pizza.

"And just as quickly as the tranquil word floats about in our hearts and minds, the clouds roll in with flashes of lightning that strike overhead. Peace goes way beyond calmness or organized chaos, don't you think, Belle?"

Belle was chewing but nodded.

## Danise C. DiStasi

"Peace is something we should all strive for within our relationships," Meme stated as she sank into the couch next to Belle. Rather than turning to look at her, Belle just listened.

"So many people are mad at someone or upset with someone who has hurt or disappointed them, and they've decided to walk away from that person, kind of like Jackie. But you've had many friends do that and you've done that to others, am I right?"

Belle shrugged, having second thoughts about going down this lesson path. *I thought we were talking about peace. I like the thought of peace.*

"Of course you were justified, right? There is no need to stay in a relationship with someone who is negative and clearly out to drag you down. And experts say you should surround yourself with positive people. But honestly, Belle, take a look back on your life. You've had broken relationships, friendships, and business ties that ended in hurt and disappointment. Remember, Mom said we should never walk down the street or attend an event and feel like we can't say hello to someone we used to be friends with. Wise words, right?"

Belle didn't respond.

"Yet I know so many people who turn away from others and even go so far as to influence their entire family and circle of friends to shun someone. How sad. Imagine the energy wasted because so much time is spent justifying that action."

"Well, Meme, personally, there are some people we are justified in leaving. You just don't get what they did. It may have been extremely hurtful." *Three years without talking to my daughter? You think that's not hurtful?* "And what does this have to do with peace? Wasn't that what we started talking about in the first place? I want to go back to the subject line, thank you!"

"I know, yet I am reminded that it is better to live as a peacemaker rather than getting up every morning, tying that old albatross around your neck, and dragging the chains along as I justify petty behaviors.

# Hide And Seek

Belle, we can't talk about peace unless we address forgiveness. And you started that process with Jackie just today."

"Well, actually, I forgave her a long time ago, not just today."

"Right! So many times people *say* they've forgiven someone in their hearts. And onward they go, believing they've done what they needed to do. But I am challenging you to live beyond that attitude. I believe people can't have peace if there isn't action. There is a step before true peace can occur. That uncomfortable step is in one small and power-packed word: *go!* Settle in your heart to go to that person. And just as you resolve to take that one step to go, you will find the strength to take the next step and the step after that."

"I did do that with Jackie. I tried to find her, to talk to her. It broke my heart. I had to forgive her long before our conversation today."

"Yes, but you held on to bitterness and anger."

Belle bit her lip and nodded.

"Remember Suzanne?"

Belle nodded and rolled her eyes. *Oh, yes, how I remember Suzanne!* Suzanne and Belle had been friends and served on a community foundation board together. They had been selected for a high-profile fundraising committee, and they had both been excited to serve. At first it was fun. They were incredibly productive and were making great strides with the committee, taking on several sub-groups together and inching closer toward the audacious goal that the foundation set.

But Belle started to see some behaviors in Suzanne that seemed out of character. At first, when Belle confronted her, Suzanne was very receptive to her truth telling and agreed to make some changes. As time went on, however, Suzanne began to gossip more and more about other board members as well as other women in the business community, and became less receptive to hearing truth.

This was a tough time because Belle had to step back and do some self-assessment. *Was it me? Was I seeing flaws in her that were truly inside of me?* Thanks to Sophie, Belle understood the need to self assess. Through this she learned that many times when she would see behaviors in others, those same behaviors could be found in her, though she never liked to admit it. But after this time of reflection, she was becoming ardently aware that Suzanne was bullying, lying, and manipulating others in the committees and that made her uncomfortable. Now Suzanne's reaction to feedback was volatile yet passive-aggressive. On the surface, she appeared to agree with Belle, but behind the scenes she would backstab, undercut, and sabotage her. Suzanne constantly stated, "trust me," yet her actions were anything but trustworthy.

Belle had to make a tough decision about whether to stay on the board and continue to serve on the committee or leave. However, if she left, she knew Suzanne would gossip about her. Belle's sanity was at stake, and it was time to sever the relationship. The committee had come to the end of its term, having completed its assignment. To Belle's surprise, Suzanne actually decided to resign from the board, explaining that her work was just too consuming. Belle made a point to speak with Suzanne, making sure they continued working on their relationship and saying that their friendship was much more important than just their working together. Certainly the two of them could work out any differences. Suzanne agreed and all seemed to go well.

Sure enough, what Belle feared did happen. Suzanne stopped all communications with her. Because Belle and Suzanne had been friends, on a number of occasions Belle reached out to reconcile. Of course, she did not get a response, and there was no explanation as to why Suzanne did not speak to Belle any longer. Belle was sure that Suzanne expected her to know exactly what she did wrong, and she would be right, she should have known. But she didn't, and Belle made that clear, hoping that if she could meet with Suzanne and listen to her side, Belle would completely understand and profusely ask for forgiveness.

## Hide And Seek

"Oh, yes, I remember Suzanne," Belle sighed. "She still does not talk to me," she shrugged.

"The stalemate does not matter. For you to have peace, you are the one who needs to go and continue to take that step toward reconciliation. This is not someone who committed a heinous crime. This is a friend who must be hurt because of something you did."

"Seriously?" Belle asked, wide-eyed. "How many times am I supposed to do that? I have reached out, and only Suzanne can tell me what I did to hurt her so badly."

"True! At some point, that discussion will need to take place, and you will need to hear. *Then* true forgiveness can take place and reconciliation can begin."

"Thanks for the words of wisdom, Meme. Now what about that peace?"

Meme smiled. "Are you willing to wait, to continue to love and continue to reach out to Suzanne?"

"I'll have to think about that," said Belle as she reached out to start eating the other piece of pizza.

Meme put her hands behind her head. "Ah, this issue is so prevalent for women. They can look back over their lives and see a number of girlfriend relationships severed because of one bad word, or a look, or any number of reasons. They start this pattern very young and hone this skill along with every other. For some, it is effortless to go through the cycle over and over again. This has never happened to you, right Belle?

"Here's the crazy cycle: You develop a friendship. You begin to build trust but hold a piece of yourself back, just in case. You watch with an ever-so-watchful eye. Boom, there! Something was said, but you can dismiss it for now. You decide, however, to see if this is a pattern, so you ask others in your circle if they have seen the same pattern in this person. And sure enough, this person hurts your feelings, and you withdraw. You let everyone know how much your feelings are hurt. You separate, and if you have to see this person, you are simply cordial. Finally the death knell: she unfriends you. Then you network and meet a new friend. You develop a friendship, and the cycle starts all over again.

"You get the idea, right?" Meme waved her hand, signaling the silliness of it all. "Some women have gotten so good at this cycle that they can shorten it and burn through friendships in one or two steps. Wake up!"

Belle slightly jumped. *How does this young lady know this?*

Meme was right in front of Belle, her face almost pleading. "Why do women do this to one another? Pride, fear, jealousy, insecurity? What if, what if we started today to go and be reconciled to the people with whom we have severed ties? Do you think that action could bring healing? You know your heart's desire is to truly experience peace beyond all understanding. It begins with forgiveness, the tiny word and the big step: go!

"Belle, you've worn that tough girl mask for so long, you and every other woman in the business world."

"Now that's a pretty broad stroke, don't you think?"

Meme raised her eyebrows as if to say, "Do you believe that is far-fetched?"

"Women get their feelings hurt so easily and move into the victim role," said Meme, "in spite of their tough outer shell. Remember we talked about the lie of rejection? Someone doesn't return an email, and their thoughts take them down a path that says, 'She must not like me,' or 'She doesn't care about me,' or 'She has other priorities, and I just don't matter.' Then women reason, 'How dare she not return my email!' Could it be this person was truly busy, sick, or had pressing personal matters and it really had nothing to do with you?"

# Hide And Seek

"Are you asking me?"

"Perhaps. How about when someone shares a truth about a character issue and you cut that person off? Or someone shares a business idea and you think she's trying to take over? The list could go on and on.

"If more people could just take a moment, step back, and realize, *It really is not about me*, they would not take things so personal. Then, in due time, whatever issue is going on, they'd get a better understanding of the friend. Remember reading Oswald Chambers so long ago?"

Belle nodded as she dabbed the corner of her mouth.

"He wrote in his devotional, *My Utmost for His Highest*: 'There is always one fact more in every man's case about which we know nothing.'"

"Yes," said Belle with a faraway look, "now that you mention it, I have referred to that quote on a number of occasions, and it has helped me to better understand timing, other's intentions, and my own sense of inadequacy as I seek to understand others. It's been a while since I've thought about that quote, though, I will admit."

Meme moved closer and held both of Belle's hands. "The reason you felt so much peace after talking with Jackie is because all the questioning, doubt, hurt, and pain all went away with the two words, 'I'm sorry.' You can't have peace in your heart if doubt, fear, bitterness, and anger are lurking around in the same space. Peace is not easily attained without recognizing the need to forgive others *and* ourselves. Peace is knowing without a doubt that God is wise, and because he is in control, we can trust him with our struggles rather than ourselves."

There it was again! That overwhelming sense of peace that Belle wanted to swim in, to drink up almost. And then she realized what Meme said was true. She needed to put down the mask of her tough outer shell and take the first step to remove fear, doubt, hurt, and anger. And it started with her willingness to ask forgiveness, and forgive others.

She looked up Suzanne's number and pressed dial.

CHAPTER 10

# Patience Is A Virtue

She knew she would get voicemail, and sure enough, there was Suzanne's curt, brief message. Belle left a brief voicemail, asking Suzanne if it would be possible for the two of them to meet. "I just feel like we should talk, if you're okay with that." She felt awkward like the words came out wrong. Sadly, she knew she would never hear from Suzanne.

As she ended the call, her cell phone froze. "Argh!" Belle held up the phone as though she were going to throw it to the floor. "Oh, this phone!"

Meme sat quietly, her hair draped over her shoulders as she intently watched Belle.

"What now, Meme?" Though Belle was still confused as to who Meme was and why she was there, she knew that whenever she had a negative reaction to something, Meme would most assuredly have some words of wisdom.

Meme shook her head and said, "Nothing."

"I know you want to tell me something," she said as she sat back, "so go ahead and spill it."

"I am not really sure you'll hear it, but let me process something with you."

Belle swooped her hand in front of her and said, "You have the floor."

"Belle, my heart breaks for you."

# Hide And Seek

"Pity I don't need," Belle said as she stood to throw away the paper plate and napkins from lunch.

"There's this incredible desperation that plays out that is so often missed. Why, may I ask, why you are so impatient?"

Belle didn't respond. Instead she stopped, turned and looked quizzically at Meme. *Is she taller?* she asked herself. *How strange.* She then quickly focused on what Meme was saying.

"Our society is so used to immediate gratification that if we don't get our food within seconds of ordering it at the drive through, we blow the horn. If someone doesn't immediately text back, we get impatient or, as we just now discussed, our feelings get hurt, right?" She didn't wait for an answer. "Remember your first job in the real world? Remember the technology?"

Belle laughed out loud as she recalled the technology in the data center she worked at right out of college. Back in the mid-to-late '70s, they had just introduced a brand new computer in their department. This technical wonder was going to make their life so much easier. The computer took up the entire room. The fan of the computer was more like a deafening roar than a gently whirring of computers today. If someone stood at the doorway to tell her something she could not hear them from just a few feet away. They would load the computer with all the information for the day and leave it overnight to process one monthly report.

"Fast forward forty years to today," Meme said. "If your smartphone freezes for one second, you tap on it, tap again, tap again, and it goes through all the movements that you thought it wasn't picking up. It deletes or forwards an email you didn't want deleted. Oh the aggravation, right?"

"Yes, it's ridiculous! It is supposed to make life easier!" Belle was very animated, waving her arms.

Meme politely nodded and continued. "Remember the other day when you put your phone into the speaker and it stopped after a minute or two? You turned it back on, and after two minutes it stopped again."

"Yep."

"OK, one more example. You can be diligently working on something online, and your Wi-Fi connection will drop, just like that."

Belle lowered her head because she knew when these things happen, she has to refrain from throwing her phone out the window or to a safer, softer location: the floor. She knows she can feel it bubble up and she's ready to explode.

"Belle, what if you just power down?"

Belle's rebellious, hard-headed, independent nature said, "Because, Meme, I shouldn't have to 'power down.' Technology should be such that it should just work, no powering down. That's ridiculous!"

But she decided to go ahead and power down. She waited, she didn't throw anything, she just waited. After a few minutes she powered back up, and of course, everything worked.

"What is it about patience that makes you crazy, Belle?"

"I have no idea, Meme. It just seems such a waste of time. I know I get frustrated over silly things that we really have no control over."

"Yet when people make rash decisions," Meme responded, "or quickly react, the results can be disastrous. Patience does produce character as we joyfully press through situations and keep from becoming angry with others when timing doesn't match our expectations. We can become bitter and full of resentment, which is expressed as agitation or anger with others.

"Is it not true that today more than ever we are always waiting? Our patience wears thin as we wait. Patience truly is a virtue, and, for women, it can be one of the greatest virtues that define us."

Belle pondered these thoughts to herself as she wiped her hands. She knew it was painful for many of her friends who shared stories about waiting to get married, waiting on a career decision, or waiting for the healing of a loved one. She admitted there was nothing more painful than waiting to become a mother.

Belle recalled her own heartbreak in that area, only to now have one estranged child and the other living so far away it felt as though the relationship was strained beyond repair. Patiently waiting to be a family together was more painful than she could have ever imagined.

"Belle," Meme whispered, "patience is one of the most prevailing issues most of us deal with on a regular basis. It is a characteristic that has to be practiced every day, and we must be intentional about being patient."

Belle sat down behind her desk and let out a long sigh. She looked at Meme and said softly, "Meme, I am really tired and really behind in my work. Must everything always be a lesson?"

Meme was silent and then slowly smiled. "Life is a journey, Belle. Enjoy each step whether it is a tough climb or a mountaintop experience."

Belle digested Meme's words as she looked at her phone and saw a text from Lisa about Carly's funeral. Her heart broke as the reality of her friend's loss came full circle. She glanced back at Meme, whose hair was sleek and pulled back in a long ponytail. Gone was the little girl with the missing teeth. Here was a young woman in her early twenties, yet it was clearly Meme.

"Meme, how is it you are maturing so quickly?"

"It's about the journey, Belle. Just remember to enjoy the journey because time passes so quickly."

Belle slowly shook her head in amazement.

## CHAPTER 11

---❖---

# Kindness

Belle read the rest of the message from Lisa asking for assistance in setting up the food for the funeral. Belle smiled and was so thankful that her friend did not use the excuse of Belle being "too busy" to help her. She wanted to help and didn't even know where to begin. Helping her with the food was exactly Belle's strong suit. She could get Jann to help her with the planning.

*Wait a minute*, Belle thought as she looked up. She called her CFO, Chuck, and her COO, Lynne. Then she got up from her seat and walked out to speak with Jann. Jann looked up from her computer as Belle opened the door.

"Jann, could you come in my office for a minute?"

"Sure!" Jann jumped up from her desk, notebook and pen in hand, and took a seat opposite from Belle, who was behind the desk.

"Jann, I need to take some time away from the office. I know this may not be the best time, considering some of the issues I am having with the board—"

"How much time?" Jann interrupted.

"I'm not sure. A week perhaps. Ten days max. I just need some downtime, and I want to help Lisa with the funeral arrangements."

"I can help you with those details. Just let me know what you need."

"Not this time, Jann, but thank you so much. I have some other things I need your help with. I have five projects on the table right now that need attention. While each of the division's vice presidents have their goals established for what needs to be achieved, I need you to oversee and manage each project. Everyone has their responsibilities and I will share more details about my absence with them, I just need someone to organize all the pieces to make sure no balls get dropped. You can work closely with Lynne and Chuck. They're ready to jump in."

Jann smiled as the two of them planned, wrote on the white board, and sat with Chuck, Lynne and each vice president to understand assignments. It was the end of their business day by the time they finished planning.

"One more thing, Jann," Belle said as she began packing her papers and the things she wanted to take with her. "While I'm gone, can you get rid of this desk? I hate that whole command-central image of the big executive desk. I especially dislike how it separates me from anyone I am meeting with."

"Well, that's why you have the other seating arrangement over there," Jann said as she pointed to the sofa and chairs.

"Get rid of that too. The leather is so cold." Belle walked over to the window. I want a beautiful stand-up desk, large enough to put other things on it, but mostly so I can stand and work at my computer with my large monitor. I want to be able to walk around when I am on the phone." Jann furiously wrote notes as Belle's energy level was rising. "I want it facing the window so I can see out, and I want a warm living room setting with a couple of couches, a love seat, three to four chairs, a few end tables, and a large coffee table."

Jann was almost laughing as Belle wrapped up her wish list. "How about an anti-fatigue mat?"

"Great idea, Jann! Thank you! So let's call it a day. I will keep in touch. I'll still be available if you absolutely need me. I'm going to head to the cottage. It is closer to where Lisa and Max live, and I can be of more help to them there. But remember, reception and Wi-Fi are sketchy up there."

Jann nodded and then her eyes widened. "Oh, did you call Jeremy to ask if he could open the cottage for you?"

"Ugh, no, I'll do that right now. Thank you for reminding me," she said as she started dialing her phone. "What would I do without you?" *And Meme*, Belle said silently to herself as she looked at Meme, who softly smiled as she watched the flurry of activity throughout the day. Belle put her coat on, gave Jann a hug, and walked out the door. It was getting darker earlier, and the wind whipped in her face as she stepped out of the office building. A woman Belle had never seen before was standing by the door.

"Ma'am, any chance you could spare me some money? I don't need much. I'm just going to run across the street to get some food. I don't have any—"

Belle started to wave her hand in the air to dismiss the woman, but Meme had stopped and looked at the woman as a tear started down her cheek.

*Jeesh, bleeding-heart Meme*, Belle began to think, but her heart quickened and she stopped to turn and face the young woman. "What would you do if I gave you money?"

The woman's eyes darted back and forth. "I'd just go get a sandwich, somethin', you know, 'cause I'm hungry."

"When was the last time you ate?"

"Don't know, don't remember—"

"Come with me." Belle's long coat whipped in the wind as she walked a block to a deli. "Let's order you some food." The woman protested, "Nah, I really just needed the money."

Belle asked quietly so as not to embarrass the woman, "Do you need money, or are you hungry?"

## Hide And Seek

The woman slowly started to cry. "No one's ever offered to feed me before, that's all." Belle decided rather than order takeout for her, she would sit with the woman and eat. They sat at a table, and Belle started asking questions as the woman scarfed down her food. She had only known poverty all her life. She was the first one in her family to finish high school and went into the army. But when she returned, she fell back into the lifestyle she had known: alcohol, some drugs, couldn't find a job, wasn't even really trying at this point. She was comfortable living off the streets.

Belle's heart melted. For all she knew, this could have been her very own daughter who, while away from the family, could have easily fallen on hard times. The young woman was definitely hungry, and her countenance lifted as she ate.

Belle sat quietly, letting her eat instead of talking. Belle laughed to herself, thinking of some of the stuffy women in her roundtable who would die if they knew Belle had dinner with this stranger. She could even imagine some of their turned-up noses, "Oh how could you?" Belle felt a bit like a rebel in that group of women. She had always had a rebellious streak, but it was tempered as she moved up in the ranks of the corporate world. It seemed revived by Meme in a good way.

"My mama always took me to church," said the woman, "and I remember the preacher talking about angels." She leaned across the table and whispered loudly, "Are you an angel?"

Belle laughed out loud, "Goodness, no!" Belle leaned back. She found out more information, including the young lady's name, which was Toya and that she was pretty good at fixing computers and other technical equipment, thanks to the training she had received in the army. She gave her a card with Jann's information on it. "Will you give this woman on the card a call? She'll tell you what to do next."

The two of them walked out of the deli together with additional food for the young lady. Belle boarded the subway and looked for Meme, who was nowhere to be found. Belle sat in the cold seat alone and filled with gratitude. Meme whispered in her ear and startled Belle.

"Excellent job, Belle. Way to step out of your comfort zone and put someone else's needs before yours, a complete stranger no less. And someone society would have cast off."

Belle whispered under her breath. "I was just being nice to someone who needed a little help. And you know I hate it when you talk to me in public because I can't talk back without others thinking I am crazy!" She looked around at the others on the subway, who paid no attention to her at all.

Meme scooted in the seat next to her. "Belle, that went beyond nice. In fact, I'd like to throw out that word *nice*."

Belle's eyes widened. She wanted to retort with, "What? Miss bleeding heart?" But she remained silent and listened.

"I mean," said Meme, "it's a great word and all, it's just misused. People cover over a multitude of bad behaviors and characteristics by acting nice."

Belle leaned back and absently said aloud, "What are you talking 'bout?"

Meme held her finger up to her lips, "Shh," she said, just as an older woman in front of Belle turned around to look at her quizzically. Belle held up her phone to act like she was actually talking on it. She rolled her eyes at Meme, who shrugged her shoulders and laughed.

"You know, Belle. So many people who act nice, pleasing, and sweet may be hiding so many different issues. Do you know anyone you walk away from feeling like you want to wash your hands of them? They're nice, really sweet in fact, but there is always a motive behind their niceness. Is that right? Is that how we want to be?" She shrugged.

Belle held her phone up to her ear. "Yes, I am one! I hate it when people do that, yet I do it all the time! But you can't just blurt out what you think of people. That's just downright mean."

# Hide And Seek

"True! But how would you describe what you did with that young woman?"

"I was nice. Why?"

"Nice or kind?"

"What's the difference?"

"Kindness is rooted in love. Niceness is rooted in fear or pride. Nice is being a people pleaser rather than caring about the greater good. There's a big difference. Nice is all about what you can get out of your nice action. Kindness involves compassion, just like what you demonstrated with that young lady."

Belle nodded as she made her way toward her home to prepare for her drive to the cottage.

They rode is silence, winding through roads all the way to her favorite place. The cottage has been her second home since she and John bought it several years ago. They remodeled it almost five years before he passed and as she drove closer, she felt the same familiar sense: *I'm home!*

"Meme," said Belle, breaking the silence. "What did you mean by kindness is rooted in love, niceness in fear or pride? And," Belle turned to look at Meme, who was dressed in a warm-up suit, her hair short, "wait, is it my imagination, or are you getting older? Seriously? I'm confused. "

"It's about the journey, Belle. Just remember to—"

"Enjoy the journey," Belle chimed in, "because time passes so quickly."

They laughed together as Meme stretched. "I think you're referring to when we were talking about the difference between being nice and being kind. Oh those ever so subtle differences in life! One degree off, and before you know it, we're completely off track. 'Nice' is all about what you can get out of your nice action. Being kind involves compassion and is about loving other people."

"Meme, don't you think you spend a little too much time talking about love? I know it is important, but must we talk about it all the time, like it is *the* most important thing there is?"

Meme stared straight ahead, her face glowing in the brightness of an oncoming car. Belle continued to look at her and then turn to focus on the road.

"I don't think people talk about love enough, Belle. But I digressed. Let's get back to the difference between nice and kind." She turned her face toward Belle, who stared straight ahead, not wanting to lock eyes with Meme, knowing her stare would pierce right into Belle's soul. "I'm sure you don't know anyone like this, but many people perform nice acts because they have such a need to be validated, to receive accolades. That's the wrong motive. Yet we think people are so wonderful because they're 'nice,'" she quoted in the air as she slowly shook her head. "It's so sad. They really are very needy and very much in bondage of having to impress others. Kindness is not like that, Belle," Meme said emphatically. "Many people, women especially, will help others in an attempt to control other people, for instance, in mentoring. Then they self-promote and tell others how much they've helped a person get into a class, how they introduced someone to another person, etc. That is just pride.

"Kindness reaches into the depths of your soul, piques a dormant feeling that someone needs help, needs *your* help, and reaches back out to lend a hand. That can be from picking up something a person dropped, stopping to help a young mom put groceries in the car, opening the door for an elderly person, or any person, to buying a meal for someone who was trying to hustle money from you.

"Those may be subtle things, Belle, but they impact other people's lives. Nice people don't notice those sorts of things because there is nothing in it for them. Kind people do because they don't care about what's in it for them."

# Hide And Seek

The tree-lined drive opened up to a circular drive with a small wood-framed cottage. The porch was wide and long with an entire outdoor furniture set, and the chimney bellowed soft puffs of white smoke. *Ahhhhh*, thought Belle to herself. *Jeremy came through for me again and opened the cottage.*

Belle grabbed her satchel and luggage from the trunk and walked up to the front door. She hesitated as she put the key into the lock. Every time she opened the front door, memories flooded her, from when she and John first remodeled this little home to the kids practically growing up here, to John's last trip. Meme placed her hand on Belle's shoulder. Belle turned the key, walked in, and immediately sensed something very different as she looked around. A note on the table from Jeremy said that he wanted her to feel right at home, so he started a fire, placed a bottle of her favorite red wine on the table and chicken soup in the crockpot. Meme stood in front of the fireplace and said, "Welcome home, Belle."

## CHAPTER 12

# Goodness

Belle settled in, poured a glass of wine, and took a long, slow sip. She looked at Meme, who looked perfectly comfortable sitting on the edge of the couch. "Meme," Belle started, "you once told me that you would be around whenever I felt insecure. Is that still true?"

"What do you think, Belle?"

"I find it hard to believe I am insecure now."

"It is as you say, Belle. Just as any other relationship, ours ebbs and flows. Sometimes it may not be insecurity so much as just knowing someone is here for you. That's why I'm here."

Belle smiled softly. She had grown used to Meme being with her. She wondered how many times she had spoken with her when others may have thought she was talking to herself. She felt somewhat melancholy being in the cottage that had so many wonderful memories as she and Meme sat quietly.

After some time, Belle spread the ashes out in the fireplace, corked the bottle of wine, and called it a night.

When she arose the next morning, the sun was peeking through the trees and the cottage was cold because the fireplace was still open from letting the fire die out the night before. She closed the flume and turned on the space heater. Wrapped in a blanket, she made coffee and settled on the couch of the enclosed porch, staring at the golden leaves sparkling with dew and listening to the rustling of small creatures

## Hide And Seek

through the woods. She had not felt this much peace in, well, it was hard to remember when the last time was. "Why don't I come up here more often?" she asked aloud, almost expecting an answer. Then she realized Meme was nowhere to be found. She fought back the desire to go look for her and decided she would show up when she needed to. In the meantime, Belle settled in and enjoyed the quiet. "*That's* why I don't come up here more often. I almost cannot stand being alone and things being so quiet."

*But you need this quietness, Belle, to still your heart and to hear my voice.* She stopped mid-sip, knowing that voice was in her head, yet she listened and nodded. *I do need this quiet,* she thought back. *Help me be OK with it.*

She decided to take a short hike through the woods to gather her thoughts on how to help Lisa and Max. When she returned to the cottage, there was still no sign of Meme. She looked at her cell phone to see if anyone had called. While reception was somewhat unreliable, she knew she could receive calls and texts. But nothing. *Wow, this is serious stuff about my being alone. OK then!*

She made a few calls to set up food for the next several days for Lisa and Max's family as they prepared for the funeral. She finalized details about catering the wake, then checked in with Lisa about the arrangements, and looked at the clock: 10:15 a.m. She decided to make more coffee and pull out her journal. With the sun warming the enclosed patio and the heater warming her toes, Belle reflected on the fact that the holidays would be upon her before she knew it. She hadn't heard from her son about what their plans were or whether she should make arrangements to fly out to see them. And she had not heard anything from her daughter since she had left her a voicemail about the funeral arrangements. "Oh Lord, would it be asking too much to want a family reunion, a Christmas together?" She didn't want to think about it because the pain of it not happening was overwhelming. She had reached out to her son to let him know about Carly's death and ask if they had any ideas about Christmas. He said they would figure something out. That didn't sound too promising.

*Don't get your hopes up, Belle. After all, you've been let down before. You don't have the time or the emotional capacity to deal with this right now.* The self talk started, and she was heading down a path of despair when she heard, "Belle, it's OK. It's all good. Thinking about spending time with your kids is a good thing, love wrapped up in goodness!"

Belle almost burst into tears when she looked up and saw Meme siting in the recliner on the porch with Belle. Meme continued, "Remember when you used to do Christmas here at this cottage when the kids were young? Oh how much fun that was, right? Those memories are indelibly printed on your heart. And that's good. Don't let those self-doubt thoughts come and steal those joyful memories from you!"

Meme looked out at the serene setting and smiled. A touch of white hair glistened at her temples as Belle studied her. She could still see the small child she first met on the subway, yet this was a woman who sat with her now, almost a younger twin of Belle's.

"In fact, Belle, since the funeral is two days away and I know you want to spend time with Lisa and Max tomorrow, let's do something crazy!" There was that little spark of the mini Meme that endeared her to Belle from the start. "Let's decorate the cottage for Christmas like we did so long ago."

"Oh, Meme, that would take a lot of work. I'm not sure I am up for it."

Meme waved her hand at Belle. "Oh, that's right, you're so busy here in this cottage, all by yourself, sitting, looking, watching. Fine, we'll just sit."

Belle burst out laughing at Meme's sarcasm. "OK, OK, let's do it."

Belle had not unlocked the storage unit in years. There wasn't anything in there she needed or wanted, for that matter. As a puff of dust swirled around in the crisp first week of December air, Belle swatted it away and looked around. She beamed like a child on Christmas morning. They uncovered all the Christmas decorations, including the huge box that held a pre-lit tree. She laughed as she opened it. "Oh we used to buy a live tree that still had the bulb and spend days decorating. Once Christmas was over, John would plant it. As we got older and spent just a few days here over Christmas, we decided this pre-lit tree would be the best 'use of our time,'" said Belle with a hint of sarcasm.

"I guess that's a good thing now, isn't it Belle?"

"Yes, Meme, it is a good thing. I can't imagine you and I hauling a big tree into that home."

Belle and Meme unpacked, dusted, and arranged well into the afternoon with little time to stop and eat. Jeremy had stocked the refrigerator with fresh fruits, cheese and other of Belle's favorites. They had a snack here and there, but as the sun started to descend, they warmed the leftover chicken soup, made sandwiches and settled in front of a beautiful fire.

"Meme, I am not sure I've ever seen you eat before."

"When in Rome, Belle, when in Rome . . ."

Their faces were beaming as they reflected the lights of the beautiful Christmas tree. A pang of sadness swept through Belle's heart as she thought of Max and Lisa and their first Christmas without Carly. She remembered how so many friends came alongside of them last year as they celebrated, knowing yet not wanting to believe that it would be their last Christmas.

The sadness of missing her own children could not compare to what it must be like when a child leaves this world.

"What's wrong, Belle?" Meme asked.

"Actually, Meme, I'm surprised you don't already know." She seemed to squeeze out a slight smile but then stifled a sob. "I am just so sad . . . about Lisa and Max missing Carly, about my kids, Christmas and

## Danise C. DiStasi

missing John. Jeesh, where on earth did my life go? Was I so wrapped up in my business that I missed the most important parts of my life? Did I really need to have my world so perfect and worry about some sense of self-worth and value that I just remained on the surface of everything? Relationships, everything," She blubbered as she wiped her nose. "How could I not have taken more time to go a bit deeper to appreciate all that I have been blessed with?"

Meme listened.

Belle dabbed her eyes as she slowly shook her head. "Just doesn't seem fair to finally get it at my age. What took me so long?"

"What did you finally get, Belle?" Meme quietly asked.

Belle stared ahead. "Actually, I'm not sure. Seems ironic to be at this juncture in life and feel like I don't know anything. All these years I thought I knew it all, and, well, I don't. I thought I had it all and, well, I don't." She started singing, "Ya don't know what you got till it's gone!"

She winked at Meme, who giggled. The same giggle she had when she seemed so much younger, yet this time it was filled with what Belle believed was true joy. And it filled the cottage with warmth. They finished their day with a walk just down the long drive and back, a few phone calls to take care of final details, and a quiet conversation by the fire.

"I'm going to hit the sack. It's going to be a long day tomorrow."

Meme said good night and returned to her reading as Belle quietly closed her door and turned out the light.

## CHAPTER 13

# Good And Faithful

Belle slept peacefully through the night but was wide awake at 5:25 a.m. "How ironic. The first morning in ages I can actually sleep in." She stared at the ceiling, half expecting Meme to drop a wallop of wisdom, but it was silent. For the first time in years, she didn't jump out of bed. She forced herself to stay and be still.

She closed her eyes. *Oh tomorrow is the dreaded day we bury Carly.* When she finally got out of bed, it was the exact ritual she went through the day before: the sun was peeking through the trees, the cottage was cold, she closed the flume and turned on the space heater. Wrapped in a blanket and settled on the couch, she waited for her coffee to brew. She looked around for Meme, but she was nowhere in sight.

After some time, she called Lisa to arrange a time to meet at their house to understand what help they may need with all the errands. She offered to transport family members from the small regional airport to various homes of people who would host them overnight. She could also help with the food setup and straighten up Lisa's home in preparation for after the funeral when all the famished visitors pay their last respects to the family.

Just then the doorbell rang. She jumped, looked at her reflection in the microwave and then down at her worn casual clothes, and wondered if she should change something. "Goodness, who cares?" she thought.

She went to the door and looked out. *Oh thank God, it's only Jeremy!*

"Well hello, Jeremy! Good morning!"

"Good morning, Belle! You are looking lovely today! I thought I would run by to make sure everything was OK and to drop off these scones."

"What?" She took the basket and smelled the delicious scones. "Oh Jeremy, how lovely. Did you make these?"

"Well, you know how much I love to bake and cook, Belle."

Jeremy was a sweet man. His parents owned all the property that her cottage and several wood cabins were built on. He was always so helpful and seemed to be able to do just about anything, including cooking. While they had sold the land to developers, he maintained the properties as part of a management company that he started. His wife left him and his son several years ago, but he seemed to be doing well.

"Well, um, thank you so much. Do you want to come in? Have a cup of coffee?"

"No, no, I just wanted to welcome you, make sure everything is good, and drop these off. I know you're busy and, although I don't know Lisa and Max all that well, I am sad you had to come here for the funeral. Give them my best, will you, Belle?"

"I sure will, Jeremy. And thank you so much for thinking of me!" Belle gave Jeremy a hug, and he turned to leave.

As she prepared for the day and drove over to Lisa and Max's, she could hardly believe that she would be attending Carly's funeral. She started right into cleaning chores for them so she could get her mind off the looming funeral. It seems so weird that Carly was actually gone, and yet while they were all working on taking care of funeral arrangements it almost seemed like a festive atmosphere. "Yes, I know Max and Lisa are absolutely heartbroken and are not making light of this. I can't figure out this 'joy' part of this really sad time," she said aloud.

*Oh where is that Meme? I thought she was supposed to be here when I'm struggling with these things or when I'm feeling insecure.*

# Hide And Seek

"Not so much about the insecurity, Belle," Meme said and startled Belle, who almost dropped the vase she was cleaning. Belle did not say a word for fear that someone would think she was talking to herself.

"I mostly show up when you acknowledge you need me."

"I'll say," Belle whispered under her breath.

"Belle, this is somewhat of a celebration of Carly's life, and for that there is an air of festivity. Oh, if you could only see the other side of heaven," Meme's face beamed as she stared somewhere beyond Belle.

"*You* can see the other side of heaven?"

Meme did not respond.

Belle finished the necessary preparations for Max and Lisa and said her goodbyes. She and Meme drove back to the cottage in silence late at night, Belle feeling satisfied she had helped her friends. Tomorrow was going to be a tough day, and she was ready to hit the sack and deal with the sadness tomorrow.

The next morning was different than the other mornings. Heaviness fell on the cottage, and the air seemed almost stifling. Instead of the sun peeking through the trees, the dark clouds rumbled over the woods, threatening to burst open any second. The cottage felt even chillier than it had the entire time she had been there, so Belle cranked up the space heater to the highest setting. She drank her coffee as she went through her morning ritual of applying makeup and styling her hair. Meme sat quietly in the living room the entire time. She looked as though she were praying.

They arrived early at Lisa and Max's house, and Belle rode with them to the church through pouring rain. She stopped wondering where Meme would go at times and knew she would be around most of the day with her.

Max had his arm around Lisa the entire car ride, and the gentleness of love that they showed each other gave Belle pause. She wanted to break down and cry right there but held back. The rain slowed down as they pulled up to the front of the church. Just as they walked up the steps, a beam of sunlight burst through the clouds and encircled the entire area. Lisa stopped and squinted as she looked up. Her face beamed as she said, "Oh look! Oh Lord, thank you! Yes! I know all is well, and you are good even through all this—you are good." Belle looked in the direction and saw a bright, full rainbow. It was the most vivid rainbow she had ever seen. She gasped at the beauty of it all and the dichotomy that during this horribly painful time there could be that joy Lisa spoke of.

Friends and family members streamed into the small church. Lisa and Max had attended the small country church since Carly was two years old. This was their family who were hurting for Max and Lisa. There was energy in the church that Belle had never felt in her entire life. They quietly moved into the pews and sat down, lowered their heads and waited.

Belle set her gaze to the front of the church, knowing if for one minute she glanced at Lisa or at the beautiful array of flowers or the large canvas of pictures, she would break down and cry. She knew she needed to be strong for Lisa. Even strong for Max. She noticed a demure figure in the front, leaning against a pillar: Meme.

A small group of vocalists sang a beautiful song acapella. Then a group of teenagers gave a heartfelt tribute to their dear friend by writing and performing a beautiful song. Belle was amazed they got through it without crying.

A young man, casually dressed, stood up and clasped his hands in front of him as he looked out at the congregation in silence for what seemed an eternity. Finally he said, "Please bow your heads, and let's pray." Belle squeezed her eyes shut and listened. She heard his heartfelt plea for peace while muffled sniffles echoed through this stillness of the church. Sobs that started soft and few at first soon hit a crescendo as the young pastor prayed. When he said amen, she felt a heaviness lift from her shoulders.

## Hide And Seek

A quiet hush fell among the church as she watched the preacher slowly smile and look out at the crowd. Then he walked down the steps and stood right in front of the first row, something Belle had never seen in all the years she had been in church. He looked out and said, "So I have a question for you." Everyone stared at him. "Can you give me a word that best describes Carly?"

There was a long silence at first, and then someone shouted, "Beautiful!" Others shouted, "Courageous!" "Brave!" "Fun!" "Loving!" "Joyful!" "Kind!" Everyone started to laugh as they shared various descriptions. The pastor laughed as well and said, "Yes, those are all right on and so true. But I have one for you. How about 'leader'?"

Everyone shook their head. Some said yes, they could see that. One man shouted, "She absolutely was a leader! Amen!"

The young man went on. "Now here's why I think this. Not only because she was on student council, ran for various offices in her class, and was the captain of her soccer team. But here's what I imagine took place the minute Carly breathed her last breath." He looked at Max and Lisa. "I know that was a horrible moment for you both, unimaginable for many of us in this room. I am going to give you a glimpse into the other side of heaven for a moment." He turned back and looked out far beyond the tiny church. Belle couldn't imagine what he saw, but she knew it was not of this world. Oh how she wanted a glimpse!

"Sit back and imagine for a moment," he said so slowly, like warm molasses dripping off a wooden spoon, "the minute the last breath escaped her lungs. She was free. She didn't float up to heaven like a wisp of smoke. Not Carly. She shot off like a firecracker," he clapped his hands, "and off she went." He flung his arm into the air, and everyone laughed as they nodded. Lisa held a tissue up to her mouth as she sniffed, then laughed, nodding her head. "That's my Carly!"

"There were scores and scores and scores of people lining the beautiful streets of gold as she came running through the streets. No sickness, no tears, no 'Gee, I've been sick awhile, so I can't run as fast.' None of that.

"People high-fived her and said things like, 'We've been waiting for you,' and 'Because of you, I'm in heaven.' This goes on for, well, for what seems like eternity!" Everyone laughed.

Belle noticed Meme standing away from the pillar now, hands clasped in front of her and her face beaming, almost as though she saw this very thing happen with Carly, just as the pastor described.

"Then the moment happened. The moment she lived for and longed for probably since she knew she was going to die. The moment she saw her savior. The crowd parted, and he waited with open arms, and Carly ran and ran. And when she ran right into his arms, he whispered above the cheering crowd of heaven, "Well done, good and faithful servant." The crowd in the tiny church jumped to their feet as though they were caught up in the crowd of heaven. The pastor repeated, "Well done, good and faithful servant." Everyone shouted and whistled. Belle couldn't help but stand as well, clapping and looking around at everyone. She had never attended a funeral service like this before. Even Meme was clapping and jumping. Tears welled up in Belle's eyes. "Oh I hope so," she repeated over and over again.

The young pastor stopped and looked at Max and Lisa. Everyone went silent and, one by one, sat down in the old wooden pews. After some moments of silence he said, "*Good, faithful,* and *servant.* Those three words, those three little tiny words, *good* and *faithful* and *servant*, all sum up Carly. And they also sum up a leader.

"Let's break that down a bit. I know we live in a world where everyone tweets, posts on Facebook and Instagram about all the good things they do and how nice they are and how they love one another. But that is not goodness as the word of God describes good. You see, it is not a mere passive quality but the deliberate preference of right over wrong, the ability to resist evil, and the choosing and following of all moral good. It almost always involves particular ways of behaving. Because God is good, he is good to his people. When people are good they behave decently toward each other based on God's goodness to them. The general biblical words for good/goodness include this idea of right behavior.

"What do you think of when you hear the word *goodness*, or the phrases a *good sermon* or a *good job*? It refers to something that meets a certain standard, someone's expectations. It fulfills the goal of the job. The sermon does what sermons are supposed to do: change lives. The meaning of goodness often depends on the context. A good book is different for different people and purposes. A good book for scholarly research is quite different from a good book for bedtime reading, and what is good recreation for one person may not be for the next.

"Goodness is something Carly devoted herself to. She cultivated it because, being surrounded by this society that is questionable at best, she has not been schooled in doing good. We all know Max and Lisa are fabulous parents and taught her well, but goodness is not naturally part of our character. We have been schooled to be self-centered, and self-centered people cannot do godly good." He rested his hands on the podium he now stood at. "Carly exuded good in spite of our selfish world and a debilitating disease that claimed her life.

"Carly was faithful. Faithfulness is a quality or attribute applied in the scripture to both God and man. To be faithful is to be reliable, steadfast and unwavering, and the Bible speaks of this type of faithfulness in four ways: (1) as an attribute of God, (2) as a positive characteristic of some men, (3) as a characteristic that many people lack, and (4) as a gift of the Holy Spirit. Faithful is also used in the sense of believing. It is a gift from God. The fullness of these blessings depends on listening to God and obeying him. Faithfulness affects every relationship we have. We all desire that deep-seeded, heartfelt, faithful partner on this journey called life."

As he talked, Belle crossed her arms and tilted her head inquisitively. *Where does this young man get this information? How does he know these things?* She glanced at Max and Lisa, who nodded their heads and continued to listen.

"And finally, *servant*. You cannot be a leader if you are not truly willing to serve others. In our very selfish, self-centered society today, Carly did a tremendous amount for so many others. She was truly a servant leader. I once heard a young woman say she was convinced that in order for this generation to not be so selfish, we have to break their hearts for others. Carly's heart broke for so many other people.

"Never once did I hear that young lady say, 'Why me? Why did I get this horrible disease?' Instead she thought of ways to help others, to raise money to beat this ugly form of cancer, and she remained involved in the community until she was bedridden.

"She was all those things. She was good! She was faithful! She was a servant! She was a leader!"

He lowered his head, and then, with a tear slowly glistening down his cheek, he looked at Max and Lisa and said, "I believe Max, Carly's dad, has a little something to say."

Max, who was a big, strapping man, stood and walked to the podium. He raised the mic up as high as it would go, wiped a tear from his eye, and stood for a minute collecting himself. Finally he took in a breath, unfolded his paper, and nervously said, "I have a little love letter here I'd like to read since I am not sure I could do anything else but read." He nervously held the paper and sniffed. "Hi, baby girl! It's daddy!" And with those words he released a heaving sob as he bowed his head. With each sob, more people joined him in his pain, and the church erupted with moans and cries.

Belle lowered her head as tears streamed down her face. Several minutes passed until finally Max took a deep breath and slowly blew it out almost as though he were exhaling a gentle breeze of peace among

# Hide And Seek

the crowd. Belle looked up, and there standing beside Max was Meme. She had her head bowed, her hand on his shoulder, and stood perfectly quiet. She looked different again, yet Belle knew it was Meme. Her hair was all white and almost glowing, and she seemed taller and even more statuesque. "How can that be?" Belle whispered under her breath. Belle was mesmerized by the sight but focused on the eulogy her dear friend gave for his daughter.

The teen band went back on stage to sing, and though Belle felt drained by the emotions that had been poured out, the song was uplifting and celebratory. The service ended on as high of a note as could be, and everyone filed out of the church. As Belle mingled with friends and family members of Lisa and Max, she heard a voice from behind say, "Mom?"

## CHAPTER 14

# Hidden Treasures

Belle's heart dropped. She'd know that voice anywhere, that voice that would sing the word 'Mommmmmmm?' as she came in from school and dropped everything on the floor. That sweet voice she longed to hear, yet she knew it couldn't be Jackie. She would have called to let her know she was coming. She wanted to ignore the voice because she didn't want to face the disappointment of it not being her daughter as she had so many times in her dream. Curiosity overwhelmed her as she quickly turned.

Her knees buckled as she looked right into the eyes of her daughter Jackie and then quickly noticed the handsome young man next to her. "Oh my gosh, what?" Her son Todd was with Jackie as well. And right behind them, beaming a smile from one side of the churchyard to the other, was Meme. Her arms were stretched around both Jackie and Todd's shoulders, and all three looked like they were right out of a portrait of the most beautiful family in the world. Belle burst into tears as the three of them, four if you count Meme, hugged and cried together until there were no more tears.

Belle stood back and looked at her children. "What on earth? How did you? How?" Belle was speechless and hugged them both again. In an instant, Max and Lisa were beside them, hugging them. Lisa couldn't believe her eyes as she looked at Jackie. The chatter between all of them was almost deafening. Belle looked at Lisa, who knew the pain Belle had experienced in the separation from Jackie. The reunion seemed to be just what Lisa needed at this juncture in her grief.

Finally, Todd spoke up. "As soon as Jackie called about Carly, we decided we would come out to the service." He leaned toward Belle, "Sorry mom, just me and no kids this time," he said as he winked. She playfully smacked his arm. Todd continued, "We flew in about the same time last night, stayed at the hotel by the airport, rented a car, and drove up this morning."

Belle resisted the urge to ask how long they planned on staying, knowing she would sound like she was pressuring them to stay longer than they planned. Lisa chimed in and asked that very same question.

Both Todd and Jackie looked at each other and shrugged. "I'll be here a couple of days, but I can't speak for Jackie."

Jackie pulled on her mom's arm and said, "It depends on how much we get on each other's nerves." They smiled at each other, but Belle was ultrasensitive to not making Lisa uncomfortable with just losing her daughter nor pushing Jackie away by asking too many questions.

Meme whispered from behind Belle, "Well done!" Belle turned and winked just as Lisa said, "Do you want to come back to the house and grab a bite?" And with that everyone proceeded to drive away from the small church through the beautiful wooded area as the sun peeked out among the clouds. Todd and Jackie followed Belle in their rented car. Belle was alone for most of the ride, but then Meme joined her.

"That was a beautiful service," said Belle, staring out to the road in front of her.

Meme just nodded. Then Belle smacked the steering wheel and looked at Meme. "Can you believe it? My kids? What in the world? I am still absolutely speechless," but she giggled like a little girl. Meme joined in the giggling. Belle remembered Meme giggling when she actually was a little girl.

Belle gave Meme a sideways glance. "Did you have anything to do with this?"

Meme tilted her head back and laughed. "Now how could I have anything to do with your son and daughter being here?"

Belle shook her head. "I dunno, but you have a funny way of showing up just as things start happening, like little treasures that pop up along the way."

"That's beautiful, Belle," Meme said as she looked at Belle. "How interesting our lives would be if we approached each day with a desire to find such hidden treasures." She turned and looked at the road ahead. "Like even before you get out of bed, a path has already been prepared for you that will get you through your day. Oh, just think what fun it would be if there were hidden treasures intentionally placed along the way. Some of those treasures might be in the form of trials, designed to loosen this old earth's heavy load. Others are blessings: sunshine, flowers, birds, friendships, answered prayer. As dark as this world seems at times, it is still a beautifully created world, and you have a very specific purpose in it. We all do. But oh what a treasure to see the goodness in the eyes of your children, Belle! What a blessing. Tell me, have you ever prayed to see your daughter again?"

Belle coughed. "Um, yeah!"

"Could this be an answer to prayer?"

Belle winced. "I doubt it. I mean, how could it be? I also prayed that Carly would be healed. How could *my* prayer be answered in one area and not another?"

"Oh, prayer is always answered. Sincere, authentic, heartfelt prayers are always answered. 'No' is not the same as 'not yet,' and sometimes the answer lies on the other side of heaven in more glorious ways than we could imagine. No Belle, prayer is *always* answered. And treasures are strewn about the path you walk on no matter the thorns you fix your gaze upon that lie on the side of the road. Look for the treasures!"

Belle pulled into a spot to park on the street in front of Lisa and Max's house and turned off the engine. As she watched Todd and Jackie get out of their car, she nodded her head and whispered, "Yes, treasures!"

## CHAPTER 15

# Together Again

The day's events wrapped up with hugs and promises to stay in touch with all the friends and family members as each guest left Max and Lisa's home. Before saying their goodbyes, Belle looked at Todd and Jackie. "Do you both have your things with you, or were you planning to go back to the hotel?"

"Well, we have our stuff. We figured we'd crash at the cottage if that's OK."

"Are you kidding? I'm thrilled!" She caught herself in not wanting to be overbearing. "Let me just stop by the store and pick up a few things. Do you remember the way home?"

Jackie piped up, "We'd better follow you. I have a few things I'd like to pick up too if that's OK."

They said their farewells to Max and Lisa and drove through the late afternoon as early dusk descended upon the land. They made a twenty-minute stop to pick up their favorite items and then continued driving up the familiar gravel driveway. Belle's mouth dropped open as she looked at the cottage. It was softly lit with a beautiful dusting of light snow and smoke rising from the chimney; her home looked like it was right out of a Norman Rockwell portrait.

"Meme?" she looked around her car, but Meme had not been with her since they left Max and Lisa's. "Hmm," she said aloud as she dropped her keys in her bag. "Oh, that Meme!"

# Hide And Seek

Todd and Jackie were all smiles, just like when they were children coming to the cottage for Christmas. They chattered with each other as they grabbed their bags and the groceries and headed up the path to the cottage. As they opened the door, the smell of something delicious greeted them along with a fire and a wonderfully warm home.

"Mom!" said Jackie. "How on earth did you do all this?" She looked around at the Christmas decorations, the fire, and the food.

Belle put her purse down and looked around. "I wish I could take the credit. I had some help. In fact, I've had a lot of help lately."

Jackie sat down on the couch and propped her feet up with her hands behind her head. "Ha!" she said. "You had help? Since when did you need any help?"

Belle looked at her daughter. A couple of years ago she would have had a sharp answer, but instead she just nodded. Before she could respond, Jackie sat up as she looked at Todd and then at Belle. "I'm sorry, Mom. I swore I was not going to do . . . that!" She waved her hand in front of her as though she wanted to erase her words.

"It's OK, Jackie. You're right, I—"

Jackie interrupted her again. "OK, let's not get into any heavy talks tonight, OK? Today was a heavy enough day, and I'd like us to just relax."

"Sure!" Belle said. "I am not quite sure what the bedrooms look like. But you can take your things in and get settled. Jeremy does a good job of keeping everything nice and tidy and adds a few sweet touches!"

"No worries, Mom. Just relax."

"Jeeeesh, I'm relaxed, I'm relaxed," she gave a little laugh and shook her head. It felt as though any minute John would walk through the door and it would be like so many Christmases past. She stopped and looked at the beautifully lit tree. Just the memory of them all together was enough. She would cherish this time with her children, no matter how quickly it would fly.

Their rooms were perfectly furnished, cleaned, and had guest baskets filled with goodies. Everyone reconvened in the living room just as Belle was prodding the fire to build it up. Belle walked into the kitchen, checked the crockpot, and took a clean spoon to taste test what looked to be some sort of soup.

Meme stood in the kitchen and whispered, "Be sure to tell Jackie it's vegan vegetable soup. Jeremy made it just for her."

Belle swallowed the piping-hot spoonful and fanned her mouth as she asked, "It's what?"

"What did you say, Mom?" Jackie asked as she walked into the kitchen.

Belle coughed, then said in a strained voice, "It's hot!" She placed the spoon in the sink. "*And* it's vegan, vegan vegetable soup." She smiled.

Belle, Todd, and Jackie enjoyed a wonderful meal together and dessert in front of the fire. Belle could hardly believe her children were with her as she cleaned up the kitchen and prepared the coffee maker for the morning. Meme sat quietly the entire time, just watching. Belle knew Meme had prepared her for a time such as this.

They said their goodnights, and before Belle turned in, she closed her bedroom door and then settled in to check voicemail and email. Several emails from the office, an invite to an opening, and a note from Sophie's office reminding her of an appointment for the first of the year.

"My God, I completely forgot about Sophie! Oh how funny! Well, actually Meme, you've been like a Sophie to me!"

Meme just watched.

"You've helped me so much with understanding lessons I couldn't even imagine. I've noticed you growing older, Meme, and more quiet. Are you OK?"

"Oh, Belle, I am perfectly OK. Does my getting older trouble you?"

Belle looked down. "It just seems so rapid and a constant reminder that I am getting older. But I, I don't suppose I can do anything about it." Belle looked up as though she heard something. "I just thought of something! I used to have this recurring dream, and I shared it with my therapist, Sophie, but I never shared it with you.

"I was having a latte in a beautiful garden that was part of a coffee shop. Just as soon as I would take out my journal and start writing a plan, the world began to literally crumble around me!

"Dark clouds were everywhere. I would get upset, but the other customers in the garden continued to drink and chat as though nothing were happening. I remember working so hard on not getting upset. It was a struggle. Then all of a sudden people started to turn toward me and say awful things like, 'How dare you,' and 'How could you do such a horrible thing?' Just then I stood to run for my life," she stopped and held her hand to her mouth. "My God, it is just starting to make sense. Just as I started to run away I heard a voice say, 'Mom?'" She walked over to the window and looked out.

"In the dream, my heart was ready to break because I so longed to see the person that voice belonged to and hoped it was Jackie. But I was always afraid it wouldn't be and today, today I heard the exact same voice, and when I turned, there she was. Jackie! *And* Todd!"

"Belle, what do you suppose is the significance of the world crumbling in your dream?"

"If I had to guess, I would say my world was crumbling because of missing Jackie so much, right?" She smiled as if she were a little child hoping for a gold star from the teacher.

Meme nodded. "Perhaps. Or could it mean you've been living behind a façade of perfectionism and the time had come for it to crumble?"

"Ouch!"

"Oh, I would say the most painful part of that is behind you, Belle." Her face lit up. "Really?"

"What do you think actually drove Jackie away?"

"I'm not sure, but I hope to find out while she's here."

## Danise C. DiStasi

"Really? Didn't she tell you on the phone?"

Belle stared beyond Meme, remembering the call. "Oh yeah, I do remember. She wanted to live away from my shadow or something like that, right? She wanted out from under my 'big,' whatever my 'big' is!" Belle swooped her hands in the air and then started to cry. "She said she needed air, like she was choking here. Good God, my expectations of her—the business—her father dying, it was all too much. That poor child!"

Meme moved closer to Belle. "Oh Belle, don't you see? Your bigness, your need for the perfect plan, your need for validation, the perfect façade, just as in your dream, is destroying your world. It is killing your relationships. It is what drives a wedge between you and the people you love. And yet I know your need to connect is your deepest desire, right?"

Belle sat down on the edge of her bed as she held a tissue to her mouth and slowly nodded.

Meme went on, "Belle, it is that very need for validation and to be known that drives others away, leaving you even more frustrated and empty."

The two of them sat in silence as Belle digested the wisdom Meme had just poured into her empty soul.

"And Belle, if you don't already know this, Jackie is a very gentle soul. She is not at all like you, and she never will be. And that's got to be OK! She wants real and authentic relationships, especially with her own mother. But her gentleness and your 'big,' as she says, clash all the time. It must be draining for Jackie."

Belle looked shocked. "Jackie? *My* Jackie? The girl in the other room Jackie?"

Meme looked at Belle. "Yes, that Jackie!"

"You're kidding about her being gentle, right? Did you hear her tonight start in on me about since when did I need any help? She's got the gift of sarcasm, and is as tough as nails." Belle waved Meme off. "Gentle my eye!"

Meme waited as Belle snickered. "You're serious?" Belle said. "Oh come on, Meme! She doesn't have a gentle bone in her body."

Meme sat quietly as Belle looked at her, then shook her head and looked at her again. Finally Meme spoke. "I'm trying to think who she could be like." Meme tapped her chin, looked toward the ceiling, and said, "Hmm, who would be the person who lived behind the façade?" she looked straight at Belle. "You know that façade, right Belle? Who could Jackie be imitating?"

Belle looked frustrated. "I am exactly who she *doesn't* want to be, Meme!"

"Right! And guess who she turned out to be exactly like? She too lives behind a façade because that is all she's known. That's what she's been taught, yet her desire is for authenticity."

"Belle," Meme said softly, "Jackie is a very sensitive young woman and extremely sensitive to the needs of others. But watching you compete in the business world where you've had to act and think more like a man, she has witnessed your gentleness take a back seat to aggressiveness. She's watched you get to where you are by having to *appear* to be tough and, well, quite frankly a bit superior to others."

"Oh my."

"Sadly, it is not unusual. Since no one else affirms people today and you live in a society where it's OK to 'toot your own horn,' people have to promote themselves. Well, that type of self-promotion often crushes others along the way, whether we mean to or not. And those little eyes that are always watching us witness this in our relationships over and over again. They see it long before we do."

Belle's eyes widened. "This whole time I was just hiding my insecurity. Good grief, really? So this is what that dream was about, getting to the root of my insecurity, letting go of the façade, and being authentic with Jackie?"

"How about being authentic with people? Jackie's struggle is because she operates out of gentleness, not weakness. She clashed constantly with your personality. She wanted to be like you, but everything clashed with who she really was and is. So she built the façade of being tough just so she could fit in with you, and now the walls come tumblin' down."

Belle nodded, deep in thought. Meme remained quiet for several minutes.

Finally, Belle looked at Meme. "How do I get off this merry-go-round?"

"Oh this merry-go-round has been slowing down for some time, Belle. It may never come to a complete stop, but it's slow enough for you to take the necessary step off. You can start with forgiveness. Forgive yourself. Forgive Jackie. Forgive Alex. Forgive John for dying."

Belle squinted at Meme, "What?"

"Were you not angry for a long time that he left you and not in too good of shape either? You pretended to be OK, but financially you were a mess, the business was a mess, and you had no idea what to do next. You were angry for a long time at God and at John."

Belle nodded and tsked. "I had a right to be."

"Unfortunately, bitterness took root and then caused your mind to go off on these trails that made no sense. That was the cause of your insecurity, you were afraid to admit it to anyone. It revved up the engine to the merry-go-round, and off you went, building that tough shell on the outside. Forgiveness is the first step, Belle."

Belle nodded and then dropped her head and laughed. "Didn't we talk about this once before?"

## Hide And Seek

Meme smiled, "Yes, and I sense we will talk about it on several different levels in times to come."

"Great," smiled Belle as she reached up to turn the light off and lay in silence before falling into the deepest sleep she'd had in years.

# CHAPTER 16

## Self Control

Belle heard the sound of laughter. Her eyes fluttered open as she stared at the ceiling, trying to remember where she was. "Oh, the cottage." She threw back the covers as she remembered her children were with her and flung her legs over the side of the bed. She looked at the clock. 7:20 a.m. "What!? I have never slept that long!"

She opened the door to her bedroom, excited to see Todd and Jackie when she stopped. There in the living room was Jackie on the couch, Todd sitting on the floor, and Jeremy lounging in the large recliner. He had a big smile on his face as Belle tousled her hair, embarrassed that someone other than her children was with her.

"Good morning," all three said in unison.

"Good morning! Goodness what's all the noise about?"

"Oh I'm sorry, did we wake you?" Jeremy looked concerned.

Belle laughed. "I can't believe I slept that long, so no, not at all. I needed to get up," she said as she poured a cup of coffee.

"We have an egg casserole in the oven," said Jeremy, "along with cinnamon rolls."

"Are they vegan?" she asked.

"Since when did you start eating vegan?" asked Jackie.

"I haven't. I thought you were vegan."

"Oh, well just once in awhile. Jeremy made vegan soup because I wanted to give his famous recipe a try."

## Hide And Seek

"Oh that's right," Belle laughed at herself. "I forgot! Thank you so much for the soup and for starting the fire and fixing up the rooms. But why? And how did you know?"

"Mom," Todd said, "after dad died, I gave Jeremy my contact information because I knew you wouldn't. Well, after you called him to let him know you were coming out for the funeral, he called me. He was concerned for you, knowing you hadn't been here in a while, and he let us know this is where you would be. He also thought it might be a good idea for us to join you."

Belle's mouth dropped. She wasn't sure if she should be mad or flattered that he took such good care of her. "You did that?"

"I was worried. You seemed pretty distraught about Carly, and, well, it just seemed like a good idea to have this place a little more prepared for you and to see if the kids could make it out. I must admit though," Jeremy looked around, "you decorating it for Christmas was a nice touch!"

Belle looked around for Meme and then acted like she was looking at the decorations. "Yes, that was quite a job. But I can't believe you went to all this trouble, Jeremy, for us. Thank you so much. You are such a caring person. How can I ever thank you?"

Just then the timer went off, and Jeremy closed the recliner with a thud, almost tilting the heavy chair over as he jumped out of it. "By sitting down to eat some piping-hot rolls and casserole. Let's go, gang!" He said as he clapped his hands.

Belle excused herself quickly and thought about changing into very casual workout clothes but decided to just brush through her hair with her fingers and brush her teeth before she joined everyone for breakfast.

When everyone had had their fill, Todd leaned back and announced he would be leaving the next morning. "But I have something I want to do today, so I am going to run out really quick. I should be back in time for lunch."

"Well, wait! I'll go with you," said Jackie.

"Well, I'd like to go too! No way am I going to have you here for any amount of time without me right by your side."

"Mom, we have something to do, and it can't involve you. So you stay here, get some work done, and we'll be right back."

"I'll clean up, and then we'll get going," said Jackie.

Jeremy stood and took his plate into the kitchen. "Belle, I'd like to remove that tree in the back that's been dead for some time. I'll have to remove the stump another time, but if it's OK with you, I'll get working on it." Jeremy was a large man who looked like he could pull the tree out with his bare hands, but she knew he was fully equipped with all the tools needed to chop down a dead tree.

"Sure," said Belle as she took her coffee to the porch and turned on the heater. In ten minutes the house went from noisy to perfectly quiet. Belle resisted the urge to tell everyone what she thought their agenda should be. She wrote in her journal, sipped her coffee, and looked around for Meme. All seemed right in the world even though she knew her children would be leaving in another day or so. She finished her coffee, showered, and got into her comfortable clothes for the day. She looked in the refrigerator to make lunch for when Todd and Jackie returned. She didn't hear the saw any longer and figured Jeremy had completed his task. She looked out the window, and his truck was gone. She noticed a very light snow beginning to fall, and the cloud cover was thick. And now she waited.

No Meme.

No kids. Just quiet. After several minutes, she finally heard a car in the distance driving on the gravel road. Todd and Jackie jumped out of the car and opened the trunk. They emerged with brightly colored boxes stacked almost higher than Todd's head. Jackie laughed as she put one more box on top. "OK, OK, I'll carry that one!"

"What?" Belle shouted.

## Hide And Seek

They bustled into the cottage. "Merry Christmas, Mom!" Belle could hardly believe it. "Come on, let's sit down for a bit." Todd carried the gifts into the living room while Jackie stoked the fire.

"Would anyone like some hot chocolate?" Belle almost giggled the words, so excited she was having Christmas with her kids. Oh Meme, what a great idea to decorate.

"No!" Todd and Jackie yelled together, then laughed. "No, just come sit down!"

The fire blazed, and Jackie rigged her phone to the stereo to play Christmas music. "Here, open this one first!"

"Why did you kids do this? I don't have anything for you!"

"Mom, just open the present."

Belle started opening a large box. Her eyes widened as she took in a breath. "Oh, a single-cup coffee maker, wow! How do you work one of these things?"

Todd grabbed the box and said, "Here, we'll show you!" He opened a box that had hot chocolate and made three piping-hot cups, adding mini marshmallows to top it off. They spent the afternoon opening gifts, looking at old pictures, eating, and laughing. Belle had never laughed so hard. She had changed, and it felt good to let her façade crumble. She wanted to tell her children all about the lessons she'd learned, but Meme suddenly appeared, sitting in a chair in the corner of the room. She looked at Belle, slowly shaking her head side to side. Belle was taken aback by her appearance. She looked very old and frail and very much like her own mother, who had passed away twenty years earlier. Belle felt a pang of sadness and grief along with something more—an emptiness she had always felt but could never describe. She looked at Meme and decided not to share the lessons she'd learned with her children. Perhaps another time.

Todd stood to stretch and said, "I'm gonna have to call it a night. I need to get busy packing and getting things together for my trip home.

## Danise C. DiStasi

Mom, this has been great. I'm so sorry for Lisa and Max's loss, and it's sad we came back together under these conditions, but I really enjoyed my time here. I miss my family, but selfishly, I had a nice time just the three of us!"

"Me too, son," Belle said as she stood to give Todd a hug and a kiss. "Get a good night's sleep. I'll see you in the morning." She really wanted to hug him and never let go, but she pulled back and smiled at her handsome son.

"Me too, mom," said Jackie. "I enjoyed being here, too, but I am going to go to sleep. There's something about this cottage that makes me sleepy," she said as she yawned. "It's just so peaceful!"

As they both retired to their rooms, Belle turned the lights off. She quietly went into her room and closed the door. As she finished washing her face and brushing her teeth, she turned the bathroom light off and turned to get in her bed.

# Forgiveness

Belle jumped as she saw Meme standing in her bedroom. Meme looked even more like Belle's mother with her deep set eyes and silver white hair, but now she looked strong and healthy. Belle looked at Meme for a long time and then noticed she was holding a baby in her arms. Meme smiled as Belle stood speechless, not sure what to think or say.

Meme gleamed as she held the baby tight and sweetly cooed into the baby's face. She carefully wrapped the beautiful soft quilt snuggly around the baby. "Belle," Meme said, "look who I have."

Belle stood with her eyes glistening and her mouth wide open as she reached out to touch the baby's soft head, smiling ear to ear. "I see, Meme. What a precious baby." Meme was silent.

Belle looked into Meme's face and saw her own mother. She knew right then what was about to unfold. All the memories flooded Belle as she remembered over forty years ago one little snap decision that changed her life.

Belle was just a young girl in trouble. The truth was, she was she was sixteen, pregnant, and in trouble. The lie she chose to believe was that her family would disown her. And based on that lie, she traveled to New York City all alone because abortion was not legal in the small town where she grew up. She determined in her heart to do what she needed to do, and no one could stop her. What looked like courage was fear lurking at every turn. She never told a soul, especially not her parents. She came home the very same day and went on with life as though nothing had happened.

"But something did happen, Belle," said Meme, reading her mind. "This little girl was not born. And you buried a lie so deep that nothing could satisfy the hole it left in your heart."

Belle's hand shook as she reached out again to touch the baby girl. "This—this is my child?" she asked through tears and sobs.

"Yes, this is your baby." Belle stood speechless as she wiped her eyes and continued to cry softly. Finally after several minutes, Meme said, "Belle, this is just a tiny glimpse of heaven. The curtain of heaven has been pulled back so that you will know you are loved and forgiven. You don't have to carry the weight of shame and guilt around any longer. You don't have to hide behind the façade, and you don't have to pretend. While you may always regret that decision, you do not have to carry the guilt and shame. Belle—you are free. God wants you to know that."

Belle continued to cry as she tried to focus on the baby's face and eyes. She shook her head in disbelief of it all, still struggling with the thought that she didn't deserve to be free.

"That's a lie," Meme said, again reading Belle's thoughts. "Don't listen to the lie any longer. This child is a reminder for you of rebirth, freedom and forgiveness. Those are the lies that you heard people say to you in the dream. Facing the truth was why the façade of the buildings were crumbling around you. And this child's voice was who you heard call out to you. It was to set you free."

Belle and Meme stood for what seemed like a long time as Belle stroked the baby's head, thanking God for the perfection in his creation.

Belle blinked through the many tears, wiped her nose and in that very moment, Meme was standing alone with no baby. Belle was panicked at

## Hide And Seek

first as though she had done something wrong and sent the baby away when Meme finally spoke. "Belle, the baby is fine," Meme whispered and waited. Finally, she said softly, "Belle, it's time for me to go."

"What? Where are you going? It's not time for that! Oh Meme, not you too. You can't leave. This is the toughest time for me with the kids leaving. You have to stay."

"Belle," Meme said in a strong voice, "it is time. This chapter of your adventure has ended, and I am glad to say you've done well. I do have something for you."

Meme held in her hand a beautifully decorated box, and showed it to Belle. Meme held the box as though it was the most fragile and precious gift in the world.

"For me?" Belle asked softly. Meme nodded and carefully lifted the box lid for Belle to peek inside. Belle desperately tried to hide her disappointment as she lifted an old, tarnished gold bracelet out of the box. Meme's face was aglow with excitement.

"Oh, um, wow, Meme. Um, is this something of yours? Maybe something you've had for some time?"

"Oh no, Belle, it was specifically designed for you. Here, let's go ahead and try it on." It fit perfectly around Belle's wrist, but upon closer examination, Belle noticed that all the individual mountings were empty.

Meme reached for the bracelet. "Oh, goodness. You don't see what I see."

Belle's eyebrows raised. "I don't?"

"Let me help you." She lightly touched the bracelet. "Belle, every step of this journey represented a lesson, a stepping stone on our adventure together."

The words, "adventure together," warmed Belle's heart, and she smiled.

## Danise C. DiStasi

When we first met, you were struggling with wanting to be known and valued. This is my gift to you to be a constant reminder that you are loved and valued and beautiful just the way you are."

Belle was silent as Meme continued. "The first lesson we learned was about love, remember? In fact, we talked about love several times."

Meme placed a heart shaped stone in the center of the bracelet and looked up at Belle. "This gem is precious and will serve as a reminder of the precious treasure within you, Belle. It is Amethyst." Meme tapped the gem carefully into place.

"Next, you watched Lisa lose a daughter and saw how she could share about her daughter with so much joy. You witnessed the true meaning of joy. For that, I am placing a special gem, Jasper, in its place" Meme placed it in a missing socket. "This stone will serve as a constant reminder of joy!" Meme warmly smiled at Belle.

"Next, we talked about peace, which goes hand in hand with forgiveness. That calls for two precious stones; Sapphire and Chalcedony." Meme placed the stones in two of the empty brackets.

"Then came your favorite lesson of all time," Meme laughed, "patience."

"I hate that one!"

"Yes, I know, dear Belle. We may need to come back to it several more times. But for now, let's understand it as one of the characteristics for you to walk out and live. That will take a very special stone—an emerald." Meme softly placed the fifth stone in place.

"Remember the young woman you took to the restaurant?"

Belle nodded, "Yes, Toya!"

"You showed true kindness. Not out of duty but because you truly cared. You knew there would be no return on investment, yet you gave your time and money. You showed true kindness and compassion. Let's place Sardonyx and Beryl in this place." Meme placed the sixth and seventh stone in the bracelet.

## Hide And Seek

"At the funeral, you learned the valuable lessons of goodness and faithfulness. As a leader, Belle, being a good and faithful servant is key to helping other's understand they are known and valued." Belle nodded as she watched Meme place what she called Chrysoprasus and Jacinth gems in their place.

"As we shared about Jackie last night and her gentle heart, you learned about gentleness." Meme placed the tenth stone, Chrysolite, as she looked at Belle. "Watch your daughter and learn more about gentleness.

"And though we did not talk about this one, I saw you experience self-control in not telling your children how you thought their time should be spent while visiting you or how long they should be here. You practiced self-control in ways I am not sure you are aware of. That will take a special reminder, a topaz stone." Meme placed stone number eleven as Belle remained silent.

"You've learned humility in ways you never wanted to learn, but it is such a valuable lesson. There is a saying that goes, 'Before destruction a man's heart is haughty, but humility comes before honor.'" Meme looked straight into Belle's eyes. "Be aware of pride, which will lurk in every aspect of your life, Belle. Instead, learn to be humble. While the world may deem that a weakness, that is a lie. It takes a strong person to walk away from pride and fear, to walk instead in humility. It will take you being intentional."

Belle slowly nodded her head as the words pierced her heart. Meme placed the last stone, a Sardius, and while all Belle could see was a tarnished bracelet and stones that seemed out of place, she already treasured it because of the lessons learned and because it was from Meme.

"Belle, when we first met, you struggled with how to be a strong woman yet not be pushy, how to be bold and not be rude, how to be humble yet not appear to be weak. It is a delicate balance, and yet there is a sweet spot that, once you find it, uncovers the hidden treasures deep within you. It allows you to be who you've been created to be. And once you do find that sweet spot, Belle, be thankful, for that is the greatest treasure, thankfulness.

"For each lesson learned, there was a treasure, a gemstone. Thankfulness is the key that unlocks the treasure. And with each lesson, deposited in you as though it were a seed, it took more life from me as you witnessed my aging."

Belle dropped her head. "Meme, I feel like you are preparing to leave forever. How can this be so? How can I have such a strong emotional tie to an imaginary person?"

Meme tilted her head to the side, "Belle, I am far from imaginary. I am very real. While no one else ever saw me, I truly do exist."

"Then why did you say it is time for you to go? Why leave now?"

"This part of the journey has come to an end. But, Belle," Meme said as she grabbed Belle's shoulders and tightened her grip, "I will always be with you. Just not in this form."

They were both silent as the clock ticked away the seconds. Finally Meme spoke. "Remember so long ago, Belle, when you were just a little girl? You visited a small church with your grandmother and were stirred by the loving message of the preacher?"

Belle squinted her eyes, trying to remember.

"Your heart's desire then was to get to know God deeply, in a personal, relational way because you wanted to be known by him. You made a commitment to do so. From that point on, tiny seeds were planted in your heart, seeds that now bear fruit in each of the characteristics we just spoke of."

Belle's face brightened. "Yes, I do remember!"

"The seeds have taken root. We just need to cultivate them. I came so that you would break through the façade and be authentic. My spirit will always be with you. Just be open to the subtle breeze and the gentle wisp of a hummingbird. Bend your ear close to hear the gentle raindrops or the coo of a dove. Always open your heart, your mind, and the world will be a continual adventure for you. Just be open! And always remember that to be strong, bold, and humble you must be intentional about love, joy, and peace. You must have a heart of thankfulness."

Belle squeezed her eyes closed as she felt the pang of loneliness and sadness in losing her friend. As she opened her eyes and looked at the bracelet, she nodded her head and whispered, "Thankfulness! I am indeed thankful for all you've taught me, Meme! Thank you for letting me see my baby and for this beautiful bracelet. I will forever treasure this and the precious memory of my baby." A tear dripped down her cheek and landed right on the bracelet. Just then, the bracelet emitted streams of bright gold light as the gems began to sparkle and twinkle. Belle's eyes widened as she held up the bracelet. "Wow," she said aloud. The once-tarnished bracelet sparkled and shined, and the gems were of the deepest colors she'd ever seen. "Oh, Meme, it's beautiful." As she turned to look, Meme was no longer there. Belle knew she would never see Meme again.

She repeated the word *thankful* over and over again as she thought of her sweet baby.

CHAPTER 17

# The Dream; A Life Of Freedom

"Mom?" Belle jumped as her eyes flashed open. "That dream! My God, I thought that dream was behind me!"

"Mom," she heard Todd's voice and a soft knock on the door. She shot out of bed and opened the door. "Everything OK?"

Todd stepped back. "Yeah, yeah, no problem. Just wanted to grab a cup of coffee with you before I head back to the airport."

Relieved, Belle said, "Oh sure! That'd be great. Give me a minute." She gently closed the door and shook her hair out as though that would wake her up more. She looked around the room for any sign of Meme and her baby. *My baby?* she thought to herself. *Did I dream that I saw my baby daughter?*

Her eyes settled on the beautiful gold bracelet on the chair cushion. She heard the words, "You are loved and forgiven."

"Meme," she whispered with soft resignation, knowing she would not see her again. She carefully packed the bracelet away in the beautiful package Meme had given her. She knew she had a precious gift not only in the bracelet but in all that Meme had taught her, the fond memories of Meme herself, and the gift of seeing her baby. Her heart

## Hide And Seek

ached for the friendship she had developed with Meme, but she felt a peace and sense of lightheartedness she had never felt before.

Belle slowly sipped the hot coffee from her new machine, hoping time would slow down as she enjoyed her last few minutes with her kids. She resisted the urge to ask if Jackie was leaving with Todd. As if on cue, Jackie spoke softly, "If it's OK with you, Mom, I'd like to hitch a ride back to the city and spend a couple of days there before heading back home."

*Where's home?* Belle wanted to ask. "That would be great!" Belle said as Todd slowly stood to stretch. He flung his large knapsack over his shoulder. "Wellll," he said, sounding like a little old man, "time to head out." Not one for long goodbyes, he hugged and kissed Belle and Jackie and then gave a hearty farewell wave as he drove away.

Belle was apprehensive about having time alone with Jackie now, not sure what to say, and desperately not wanting to push her away. "Mom, can I borrow your laptop?"

"Sure! Anything I can help you with?" Belle said, hoping she would say she was looking for a job in the city.

"Well," she said as she lifted the screen. "Todd and I found a stray dog yesterday. It had been outside on it's own for a long time, you could tell, but it came right up to me when I approached it." Jackie's face had a look that Belle had never seen before or perhaps never took time to notice. Then Belle remembered Meme's words about Jackie being so gentle.

Her fingers were flying over the keyboard. "We picked it up, and even though I sooooo wanted to bring it home, we ended up taking it to the county shelter. I'm checking to see if it's been claimed."

"I didn't know that happened. Was that yesterday?"

"Hmm," Jackie mumbled, "look, here he is!" Her face lit up like a child at Christmas as she turned the laptop for Belle to see. There he was, a puny little beagle with big brown eyes and the saddest expression.

"I'm thinking of going over there today and offering to foster him," she said enthusiastically as she turned the laptop around and began typing.

"Whoa! Wait! What? Fostering? Where? How?"

Jackie started laughing. "Mom, can you speak in complete sentences?" she said as she mocked a phrase Belle had used many times during her childhood years. "Relax, you don't have to do anything with this. I've got this."

While Jackie was making phone calls, sipping coffee, and responding to emails about the dog, Belle decided to call Alex, the chairman of the board. She stepped into her bedroom to make the call. Alex answered right away. "Well hello, Belle." His voice had an air of superiority. "Good to hear from you. What can I do for you today?"

Belle stopped and thought briefly about disconnecting but decided to press through. "Hello, Alex." She paused. "I've thought a lot about the conversation we had. I'm wondering if it might be a good idea for us, the entire board, to come together and do a brainstorming session about all the options available for us as we continue to move forward."

"Belle," he said with a drawl. "We already did that, remember, in the strategy session last year? We have the options outlined. I think we just—"

"Then we need to review and refine. I'd love for the board to hear your ideas." She wasn't sure what made her say that, but she put it out there.

Alex was silent and then he clicked his tongue. She could just see him roll his eyes. "Well, I suppose that would be a good idea." Belle knew it killed him to say that.

"Thanks, Alex. Do you mind if I have Jann get a hold of the board members to get this set up before we all take off for Christmas?" She had to giggle at the thought that she had already had Christmas.

# Hide And Seek

"No, that'll be fine. I look forward to it." Click!

Belle looked at the phone, admitting she didn't feel like making that call a few minutes ago, but one of the many things she learned from Meme was it is not about your feelings when you need to do the right thing. Making the phone call was the right thing regardless of how she felt.

When she walked out to the living room, Jackie was dressed and ready to go. "Mind if I borrow the car?"

"How about I go with you?"

"Great, let's go!"

Jackie had a notebook in hand and looked like she was on a mission. "Mom, now don't worry, fostering is temporary. Let's just check this little guy out, and we'll go from there."

*Right*, Belle thought to herself. *How many reluctant dog owners have heard that from their child?* Once again, Belle resisted the urge to react by rolling her eyes. As Jackie drove to the shelter, she was so animated and full of life, Belle could hardly temper her enthusiasm. However, being Belle, the self-talk started spinning in her head: *She has got to be kidding! I hope she has a plan. This dog cannot, I mean can*not *stay with me. I am not at all prepared to have a dog in my home. Why would she do this? You know as soon as I ask questions, off we go—*

"Mom!" There was that voice again, peeking into her private tornado of thoughts. "Mom!"

"Oh," Belle jumped, "goodness! Sorry, I was thinking of something. What were you saying?"

"I said that, if possible, I would foster this little guy for a bit. I talked to the shelter, and they said he is so afraid that no one can get near him. That I was able to even get close to him was a miracle." She shook her head and beamed a smile Belle had not seen in years. Belle remembered what Meme had said about her having a gentle soul. *Gentle indeed*. Belle rested her head back and emptied her mind of all the possibilities or disasters that could happen and just stayed in the moment with her daughter.

She remembered the last words of Meme: "I will always be with you. Just not in this form. Be open to the subtle breeze and the gentle wisp of a hummingbird. Bend your ear close to hear the gentle raindrops or the coo of a dove. Just always open your heart and your mind and the world will be a continual adventure for you. Just be open! And always remember that to be strong, bold, and humble, you must be intentional about love, joy, and peace. You must have a heart of thankfulness."

They picked up the dog, stopped at the pet store to pick up supplies, and went home to settle in for a day of figuring out the dog's temperament. Belle drove as Jackie held the dog all the way home. The dog was anxious when they first came to pick him up but settled nicely into Jackie's arms.

They made a fire that evening and talked as though nothing had ever happened between them, yet there was still a noticeable chill. "Mom, I'd like to go back to the city, but if having this pup with us will cause you any angst, maybe I will stay here for a few days and see how he does. I do plan on going back home because I'm just not quite ready to call this home. We—you and me—well, we still have a little work to do. But let me get this little guy settled, and let's just go from there."

"Well, I plan to go back to the city tomorrow. I need to get back. Honestly, I am not sure if my apartment in the city is suitable for a dog. So you can decide what you'd like to do. Either way, we'll make do."

Belle walked into her bedroom to put her slippers on and glanced at the gift box from Meme. She opened the box and pulled out a handwritten note that had not been there before. "Oh, Meme . . ."

# Hide And Seek

Dear Belle,

There is so much to unpack with all that we've learned during our time together. Just remember that on your continued journey, if you remain diligent, there is a sweet spot that allows you to walk in harmonious balance: strength without being pushy, boldness without overpowering others, and humility without appearing weak. Your quest for that sweet spot will lead you on a journey of struggle and change, which can be difficult and yet incredibly freeing and rewarding, as you have already seen.

Don't stop short of finding this sweet spot. If you do, a "driving force" will take over, and you'll once again feel that if you don't propel yourself to the top, running over others along the way, then you simply will not survive. And you will once again don a mask to hide behind. That mask is the lie you and so many others today have bought into. Belle, the antidote to being pushy, rude, and weak is simply <u>love</u>, <u>joy</u>, and <u>peace</u>.

It takes strength to love others. Love is the ultimate test of strength. This is the deepest desire of every being. When you truly love others, you care more about them than you do about yourself. It is nearly impossible to be pushy with them. Instead, you care more about <u>serving</u> them.

When we think of boldness, we think of someone blasting on the scene, taking a stand, and being brave. Tip that boldness over the edge a bit, and you end up running over others and being rude. Joy is our elated response to experiences in life, even when life is tough. It is our response and deep satisfaction when we are able to serve others, not as an obligation but because our heart prompts us to do so. When we have true joy in our heart, rudeness cannot emerge.

Humility is the toughest characteristic to maintain, but once you have it, inner peace is yours. And when you're at peace, it doesn't matter if someone thinks you are weak.

Belle, you are so loved. Remember that each time you look at this bracelet. Remain open and be prepared to learn more about

Love, Joy, and Peace!

"Hmm, wonder why she didn't sign her name." Belle smiled as she looked at the words *Love, Joy,* and *Peace*. "That is her name!"

Belle pulled out the bracelet and put it on. It was breathtakingly beautiful. She decided to keep it on. If ever she needed Meme, it would be now. She felt as though she were slipping back into her old ways. The bracelet and the note would be a constant reminder.

As she stared at the bracelet, she felt a slight tickling at her ankle. She looked down to see the scrawny little dog licking her and looking up with his big brown eyes. She picked him up and held him. "Listen, Belle!" she could hear Meme say. "Just be open!" She leaned down to nuzzle closer and closed her eyes. "I'm listening."

She walked out to the living room with the dog in her arms. Jackie was sitting on the floor, staring into the fire. She looked up at Belle and the dog and smiled. Belle smiled and leaned down to place the dog in her arms. "I think I have room for that little guy in my place back in the city, at least for a little bit. Now you, well, you might have to sleep out on the fire escape."

Jackie laughed, holding the dog close. "Mom, that is a beautiful bracelet! Where did you get that?"

"Well, that's a very long story. By the way, have you decided what to name this pup? Wait, are you allowed to name it? What if someone claims the dog and you have to give him back? Oh, that is an awful thought. See, this is why I don't have dogs—too much emotion wrapped up in them."

"Mom!" Jackie said sharply and went back to petting the dog. "Amore.'"

"Amore, you mean like love?"

"Yep. Perfect, don't you think?"

"Love," Belle whispered. "Yes, Amore is perfect."

"Now, about the story of the bracelet?" Jackie leaned back against the couch with Amore in her arms.

Belle closed her eyes and prayed silently. Now was as good of a time as any to share about her abortion and forgiveness and all that she had learned from Meme about being intentional to live out each characteristic she experienced.

# The Rest Of The Story

Dear Friend!

Thank you for taking the time to read Hide And Seek. This letter is specifically for you from my heart. It is raw, unedited, and as authentic as it gets.

Belle is a fictional character, a figment of my imagination, yet she is someone I know. I'm sure she is someone you know. She could be you.

As I journey through my "more mature" years, I lovingly reflect on my earlier days as a mom, a daughter, sister, friend and career women. At the age of 28, I was given an opportunity in the corporate world without knowing anything about business. I knew Nuclear Medicine so I was hired as a Nuclear Sales Specialist selling medical equipment and consequently, thrown to the wolves. I was strong willed enough that I knew I could make it and through many difficult trials, I actually became a very good sales rep.

While the skillset and business acumen grew exponentially, my behavior also changed. I became prideful and uncaring about others. I was easily angered and would lash out. I struggled with doubt and feared that people would think I wasn't really a good sales rep. But that was a lie and the fear was unfounded.

## Danise C. DiStasi

Pride took over and was rooted in self-centeredness. Sadly, the consequences can have an ongoing ripple effect.

If you looked at me or even interacted with me, you would never know those struggles were going on inside. The further up I moved in business, the more prevalent these self-doubts became and in order to mask my deepest fears, I operated in pride. The world saw a very strong and bold woman, but in reality I was pushy, rude and weak. I thought anyone who ever admitted mistakes was weak. Oh how wrong I was.

It was a vicious cycle and I needed to get off. It wasn't until many years later that I realized it was all rooted in one little lie: I was not worthy [You can fill in the blank for you: I was not worthy of love, I was not worthy of true friendships, etc.]. And that lie was buried many years ago yet continued to foster fear and pride.

I was 16 years old when I entered my senior year of high school. Not long after, I met a boy and we fell in love. I became pregnant and the only place I knew that could help me was planned parenthood. I had no idea what my options were but one thing I knew for certain, I could *not* tell my parents. I knew they would be mortified, disappointed, and heartbroken. For all I knew, I would be cast out from my family.

I quickly schemed and planned to fly to New York to have an abortion. It was 1972 and abortion was not legal in Ohio. With all the money I made working a small job and Billy's money, I went to the Delta Airline office Downtown, bought a ticket and set the wheels in motion. While the truth was I was pregnant and in trouble, the lie I believed was my family would shun me. And though that may happen to many young women, forty years later, I now realize that would have never happened to me with my family, yet I chose to believe the lie.

# Hide And Seek

I went to a party on a Saturday evening, stayed over at a friends house, gave her a list of items to buy for me on the "shopping" day we were planning, and off to the airport I went, early on a Sunday morning.

The events that unfolded that day are for another story. I arrived home that evening with my bags of shopping, went straight to bed, got up the next day, put on my Catholic girl uniform and went to school to protest Roe vs. Wade. I buried the lie so deep a fortress was quickly set in place around my heart. I ignored everyone that ever spoke about abortion or unborn babies. I brushed away the pangs that whispered, "Perhaps it was a baby."

It wasn't until many years later when I had an ultrasound exam when I was ten weeks pregnant with my daughter Marisa that it hit me…I killed a baby. And that rocked my world. I ran from that thought and buried myself in my career, my image and success. My need for attention and validation were stifling but I needed to know I was ok, that I was worthy so I sought to fulfill that need through empty relationships and a career. Yet in my heart I knew that anyone who would scheme to kill a baby and hide it from her family was not worthy of anything. The lie continued to swirl and erupt at various times in my life.

In 1990, I finally understood love. I understood that Jesus came to this earth in the form of a baby, died and rose again so I could be free from all the guilt and shame of living in a fallen world. I understood a true and authentic relationship with Jesus, yet I once again chose to believe a lie…that Jesus could never forgive me for having an abortion.

In 1997, after my parents had both passed without ever knowing about my abortion, I believe God gave me a beautiful picture of forgiveness. As I was sitting with my daughter at our kitchen table, I envisioned my mom, who had passed a year earlier, standing there as vivid as my daughter sitting right across the table from me. She was beautiful, radiant, and standing there looking at me. In her arms was a beautiful baby. My mom, who never said a word while standing there, looked as though she were saying, "Look who I have."

My mom was holding her first grandchild! The veil of guilt and shame was lifted, the need for validation was crushed and I *knew* I was forgiven. I only need God's validation. The freedom felt since has been incredible.

You don't need to go through an abortion to feel any guilt and shame. You may have other hidden secrets; an affair, cheating in business, treating someone unfairly that cost them their job, gossiping, lying. You probably feel guilty about how you talked to your kids this morning, or brushing off that friend, or what someone did to you as a child. God did not create us to mope around, walking in guilt and shame as though that prompts him to help us. Jesus loves you and died for you so that you can be free to live an abundant life he has created you for. The place to begin is to ask him for forgiveness, trust that he has forgiven you, and ask that he help you walk out a life of faith.

And while we would love to be strong, bold and humble, we can't do it in our own power. We need the Holy Spirit to help us. Once you build a trusting relationship with Christ, the seeds of the fruit of the spirit (Galatians 5:22,23) are planted in you. It is up to you to be intentional about walking in love, joy, peace patience, kindness, goodness, faithfulness, gentleness and self-control.

If you would like to take a step of faith and learn more about a relationship with Jesus and how to walk in the fruit of

## Hide And Seek

the spirit, please go to our website di-advisors.com and fill out the contact form. We will be more than happy to help you.

Thank you again for reading this story. I am blessed to know you've made it this far and that this is just the beginning of a life of freedom for you.

*Love,*
*Danise*

Thank you to the many women who have come alongside me in business over the years. Many of you have left an indelible print in my mind and on my heart—thank you!

Thank you to my family who loves me—my craziness and all!

To my sistahs Tere, Sheila, Ruby, Lisa and Judy—thank you for your honesty and love.

And to my Hidden Treasures' Women's Group: Alicia Tidwell, Amy Grieme, Callae Sutton, Caroline Weltzer, Connie McWilliams, Cynthia Lamb, Michelle Thompson, Dale Silver, DeAsa Nichols, Debbie Simpson, Deborah Yerkes, Jackie Glaser, Jane Burke, Jean Mabry, Joanne Westwood, Julie Mueller, Leisa Mulcahy, Lynne Ruhl, Mary Sanderson, Penny Cook, Sandra McIntosh, Sharon "Chip" Harrison, and Tracy Ruberg. Your love and encouragement spurred me on with this project. Thank you for letting me process and discuss these characteristics, what they each mean to us as businesswomen, and how we truly can achieve the much needed balance of being strong, not pushy; bold, not rude; and humble not weak! You are all living examples that the perfect balance, hence the sweet spot, can truly be achieved.

## Danise C. DiStasi

Thank you Lord, for the opportunity to make an impact in women's lives. I do not take it lightly the call you have on my life and I cannot do it without YOU!

Danise DiStasi grew up in Cincinnati, Ohio and graduated from Xavier University with a degree in Radiologic Science and licensed in Nuclear Medicine. She spent 27 years in the medical industry in a number of positions such as Nuclear Product Specialist, Corporate Account Manager and Vice President of Sales and Marketing.

She joined The Ken Blanchard Companies in 2001and focused on business development, facilitating, and training and was involved with Ken's Lead Like Jesus ministry.

Since 2004, she has been consulting and coaching in leadership and business development and is currently President and Chief Relationship Officer of DiStasi Advisors, LLC. Building on her success over the years by helping companies grow, she has coached Fortune 500 C-Level executives and their teams on leadership, character development, productivity, performance, and team building solutions.

Danise enjoys writing, speaking, being Nonna to her two grandchildren, working out, relaxing with her family, gardening, and gleaning wisdom from Louie, her rescued pup, who has enriched her life immensely!

Contact di-advisors.com to inquire about speaking engagements, small groups, and study guides.